COLORING BOOK

CLOTIHNG ANIMALS

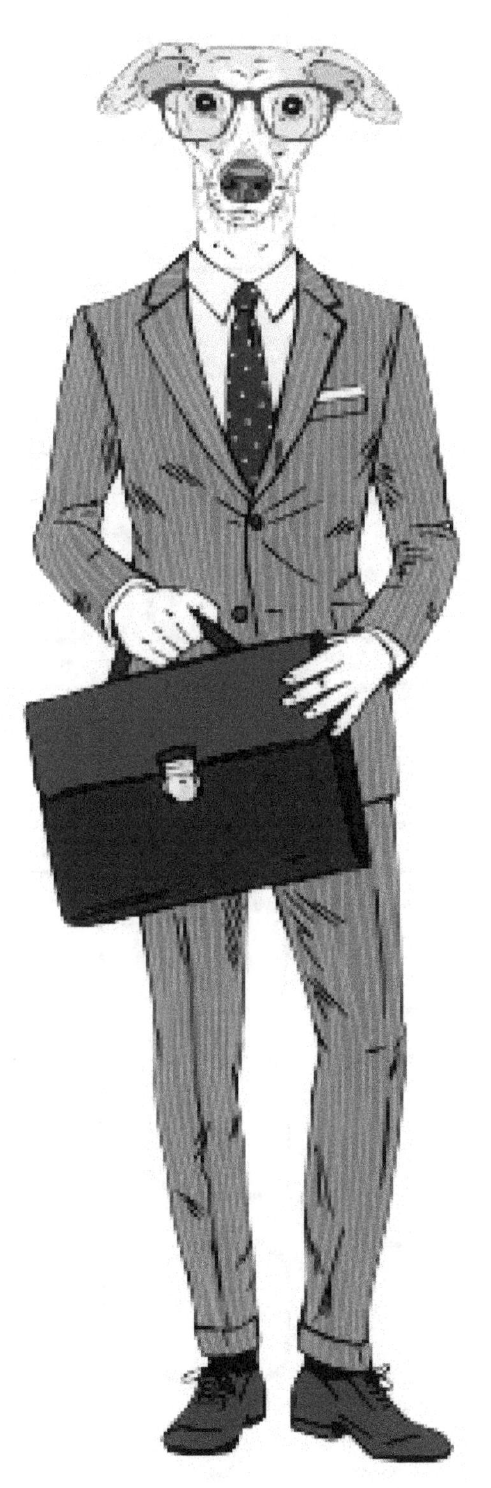

Color Test Pages

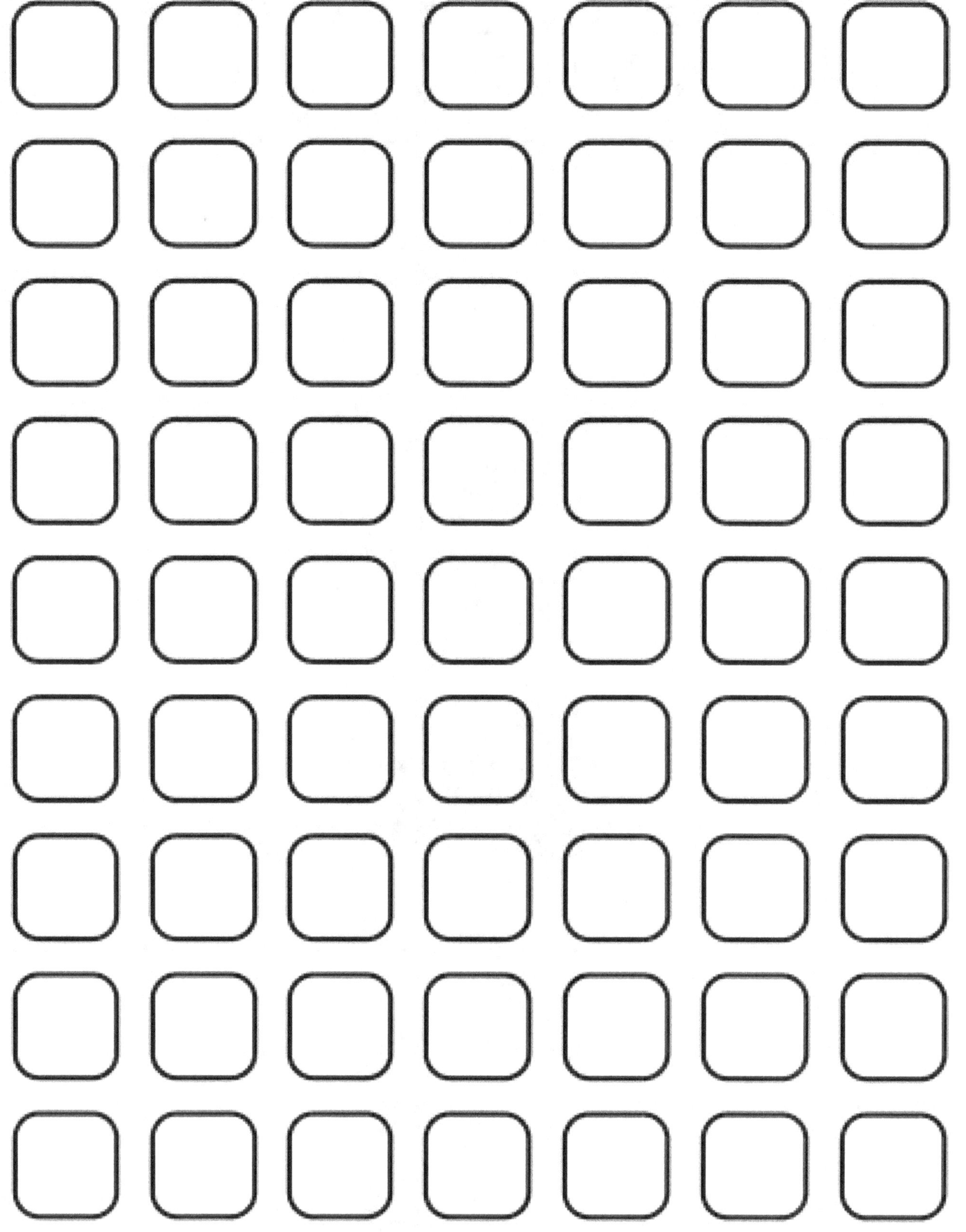

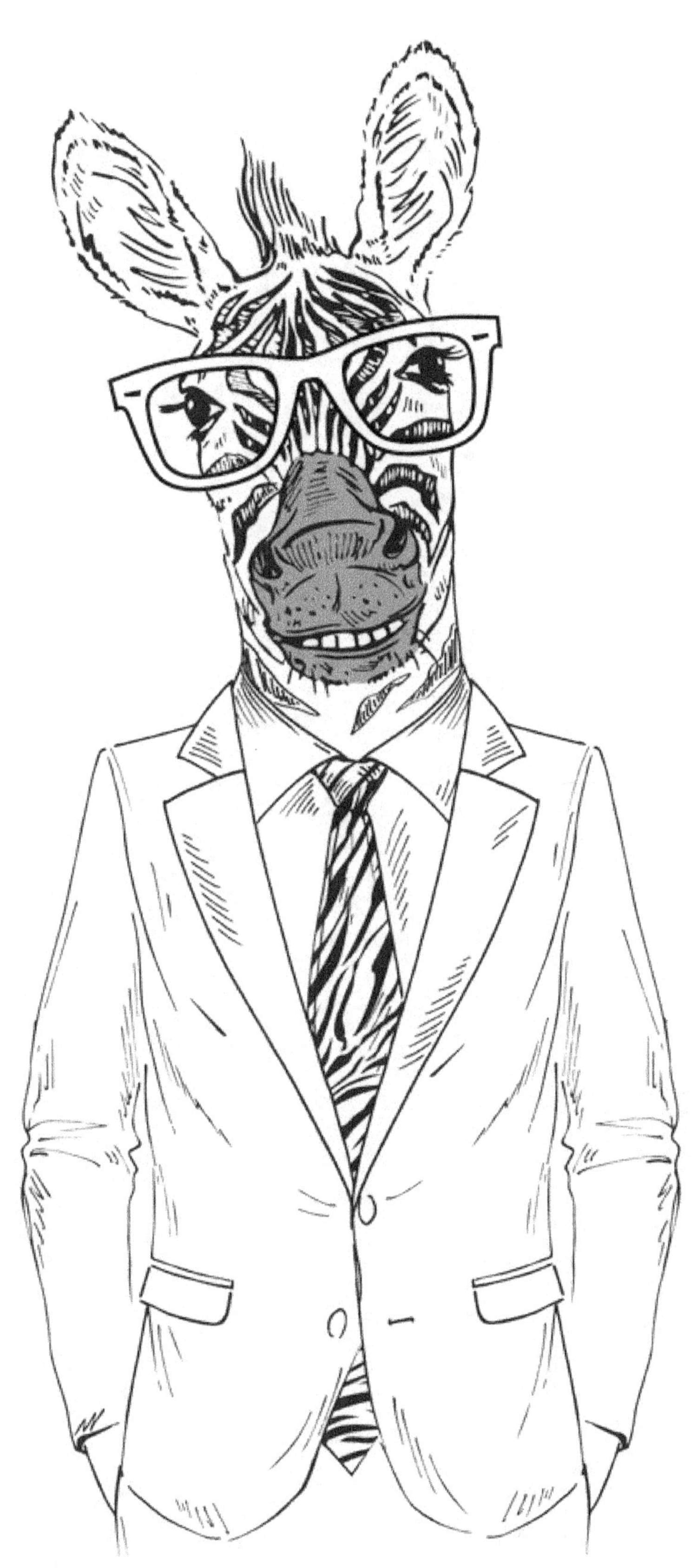

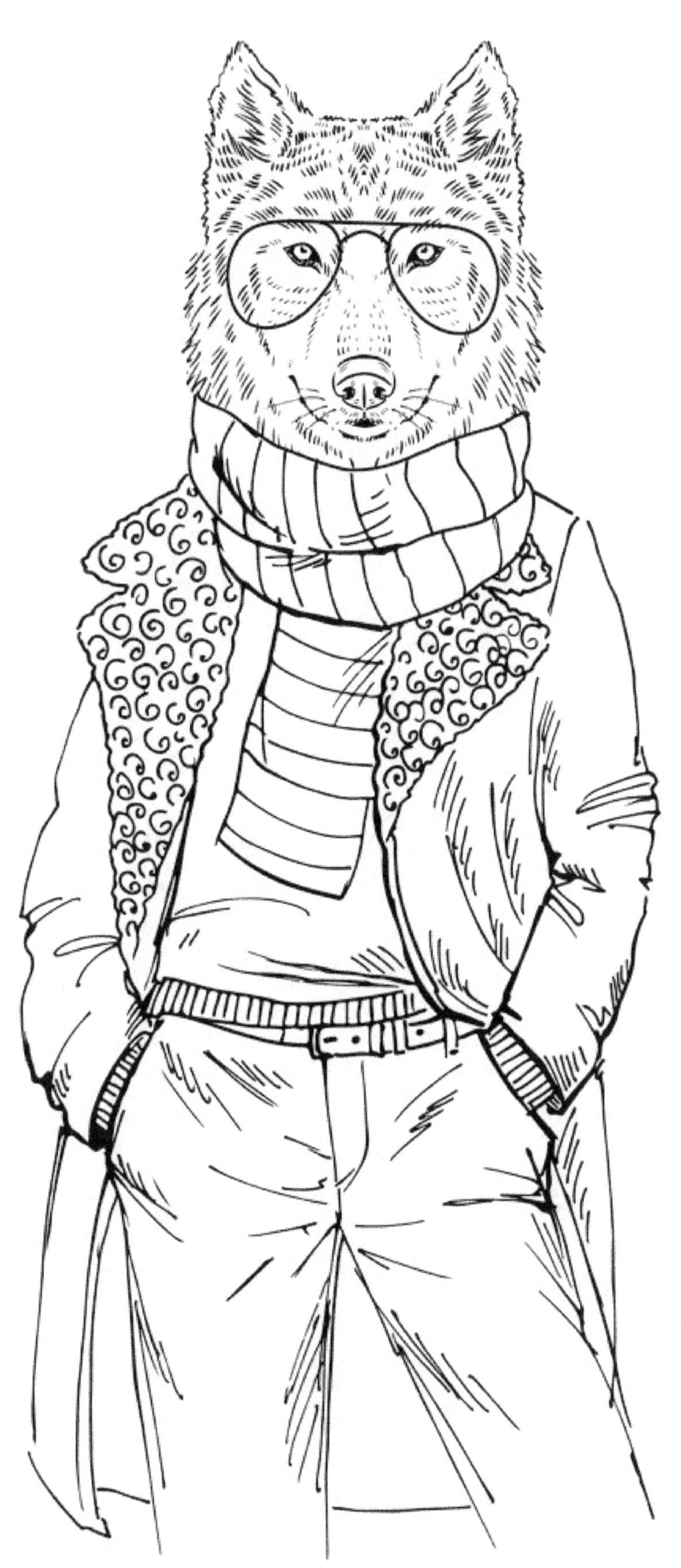

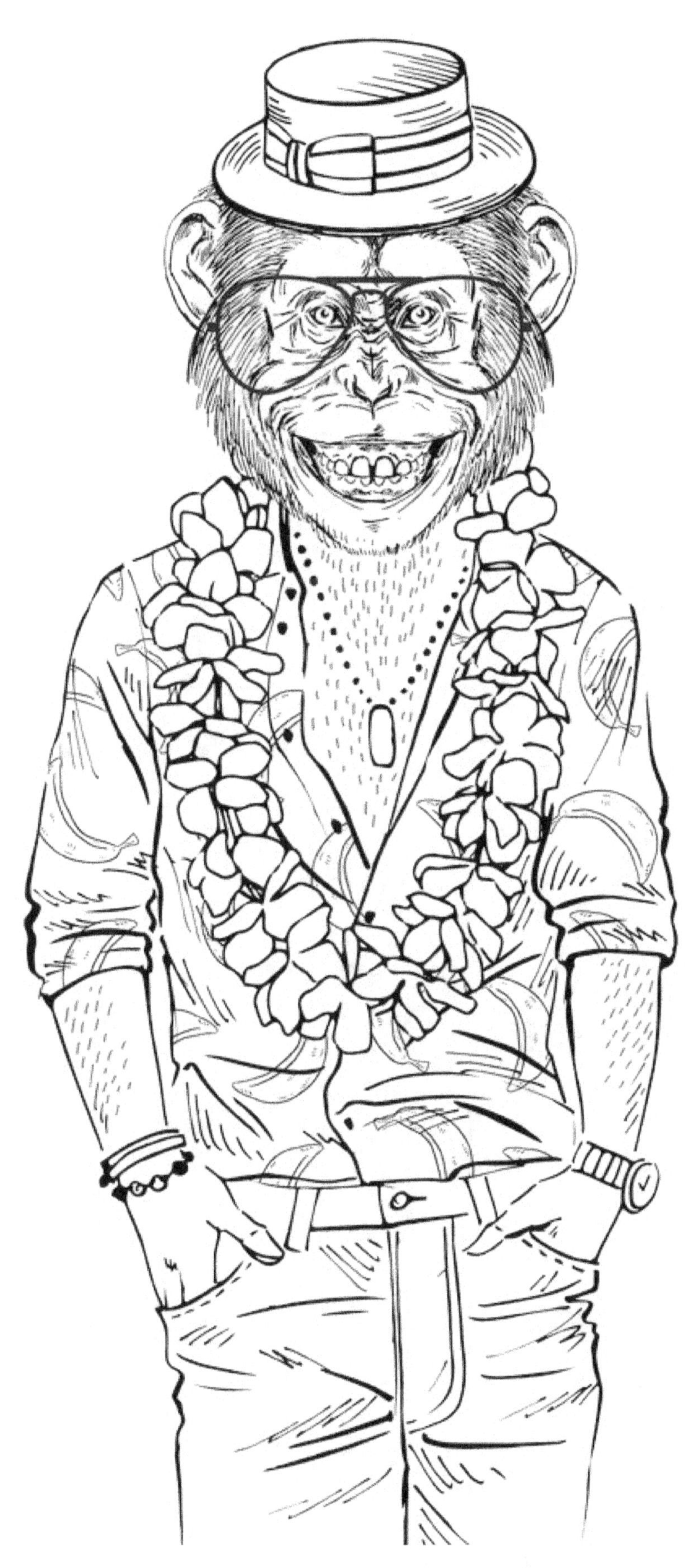

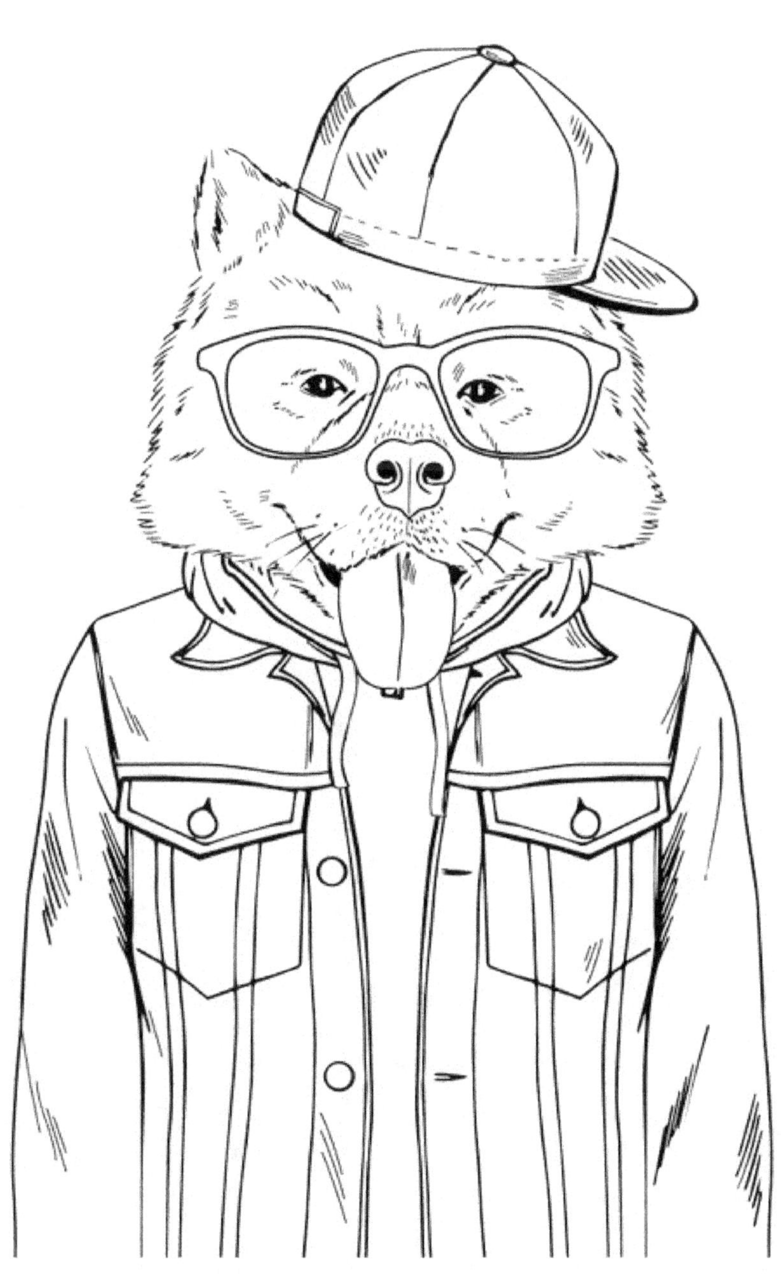

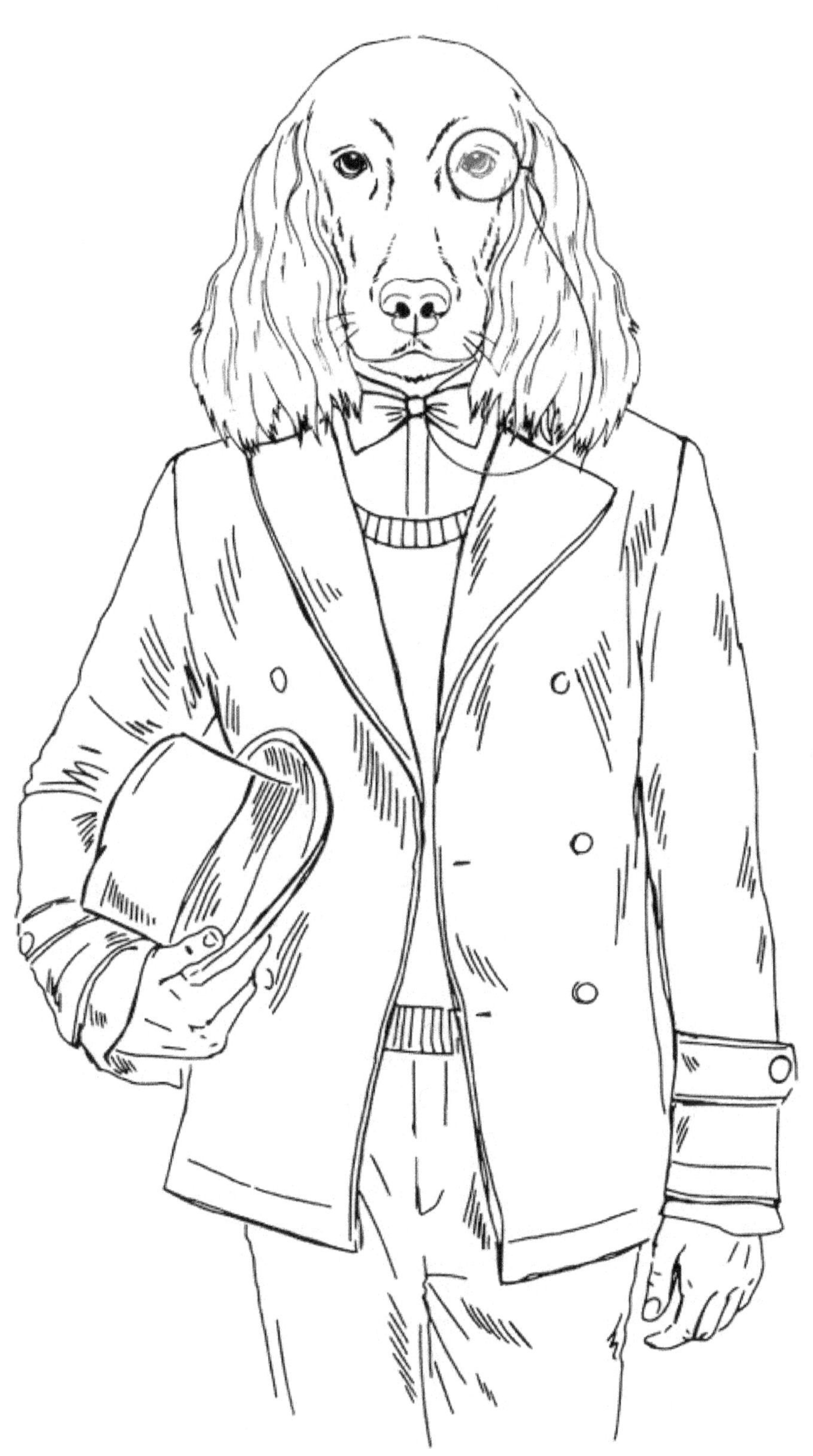

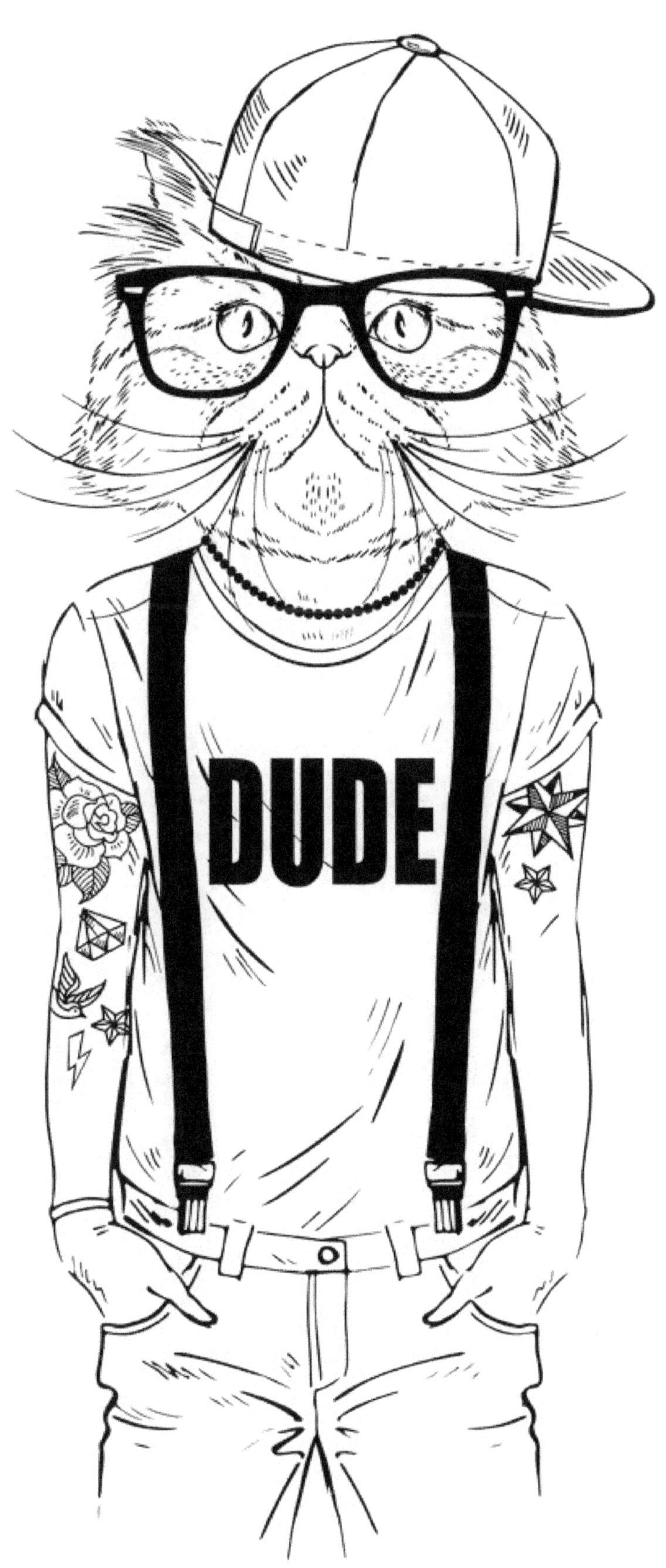
DUDE

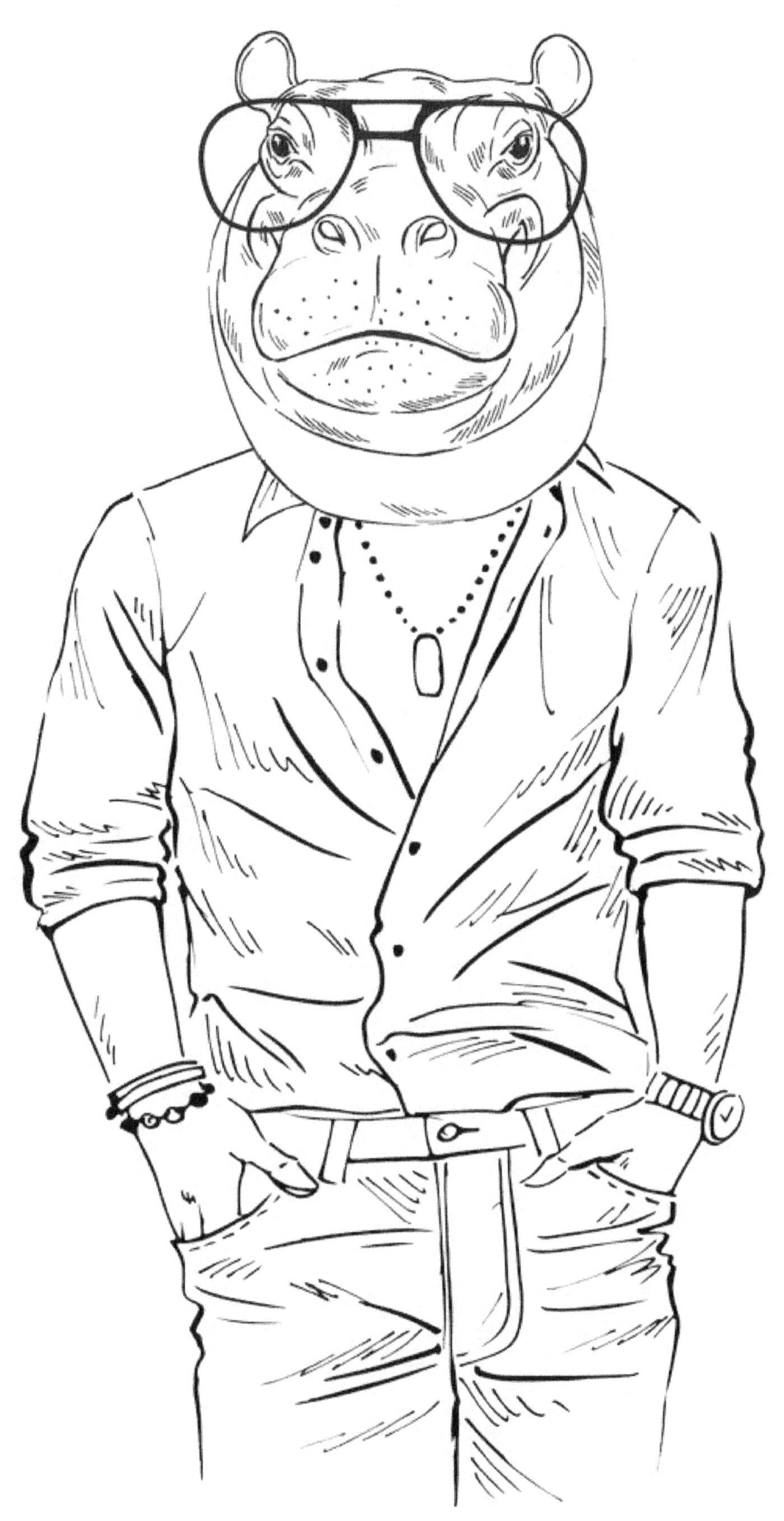

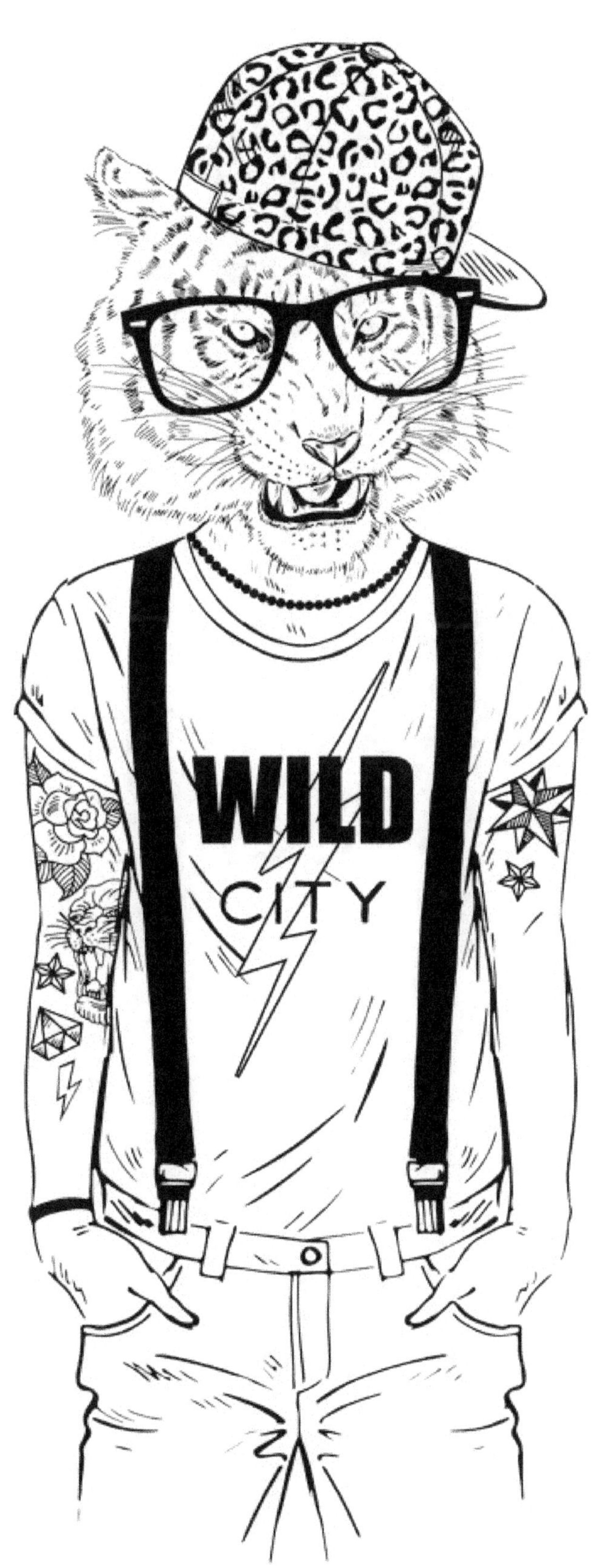

WILD
CITY

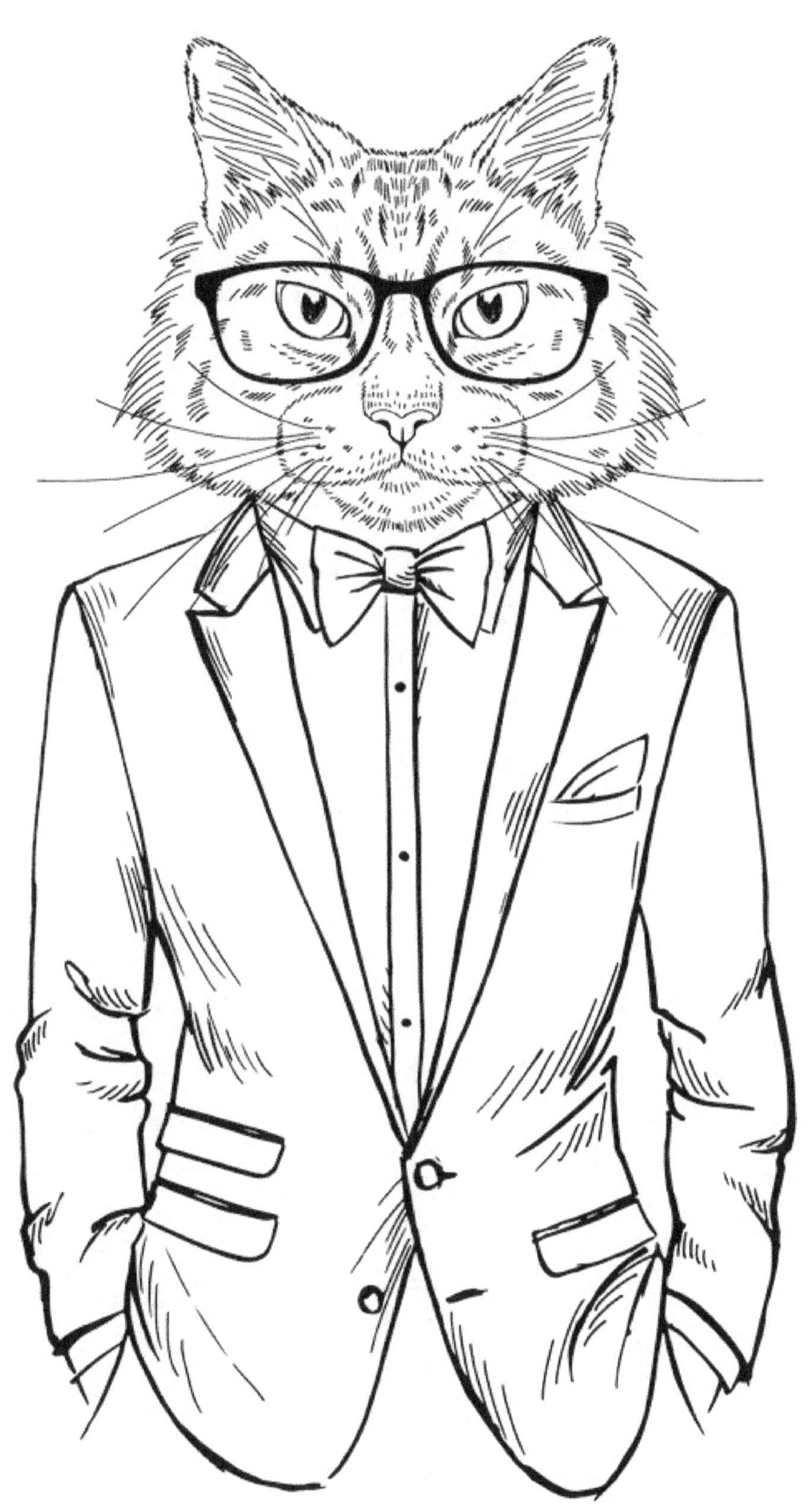

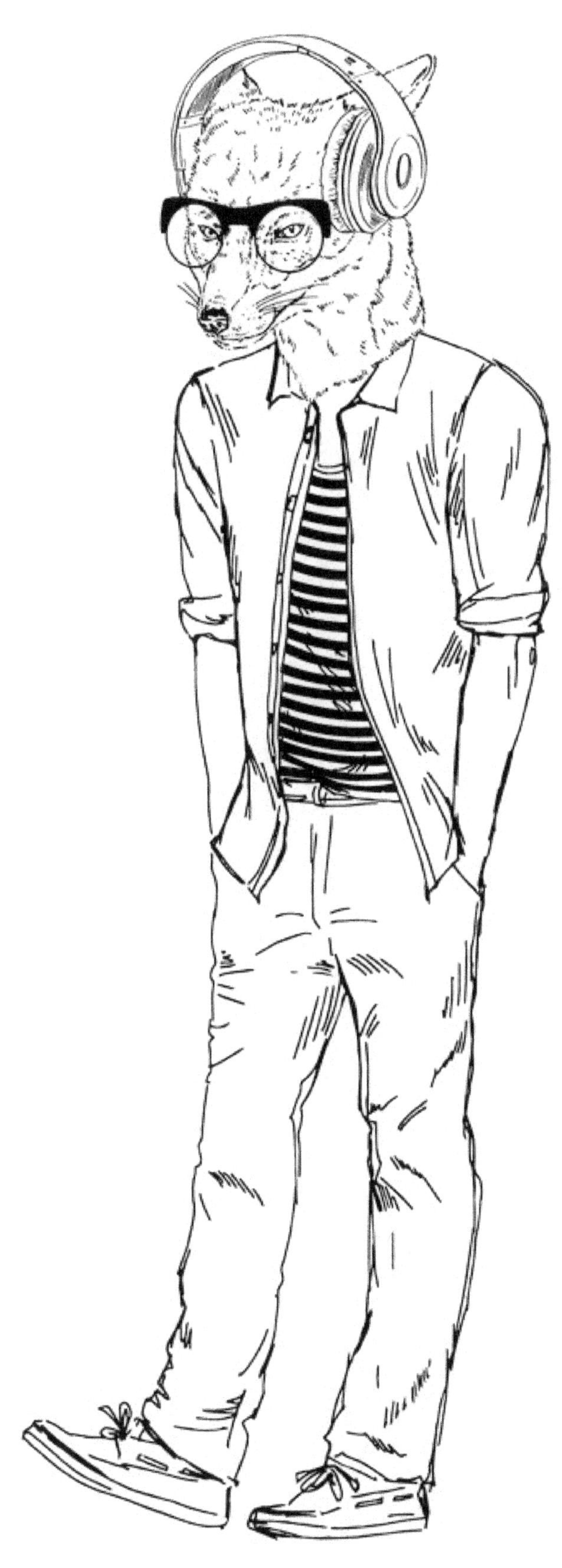

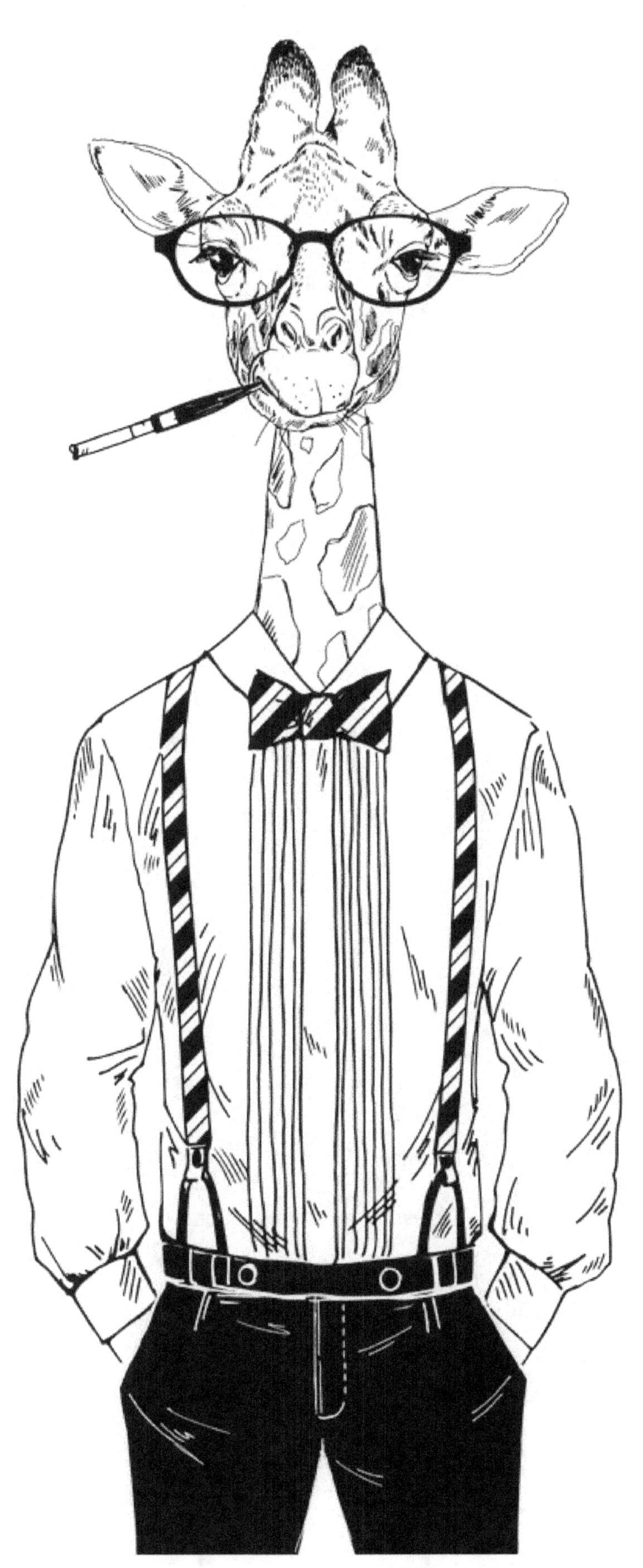

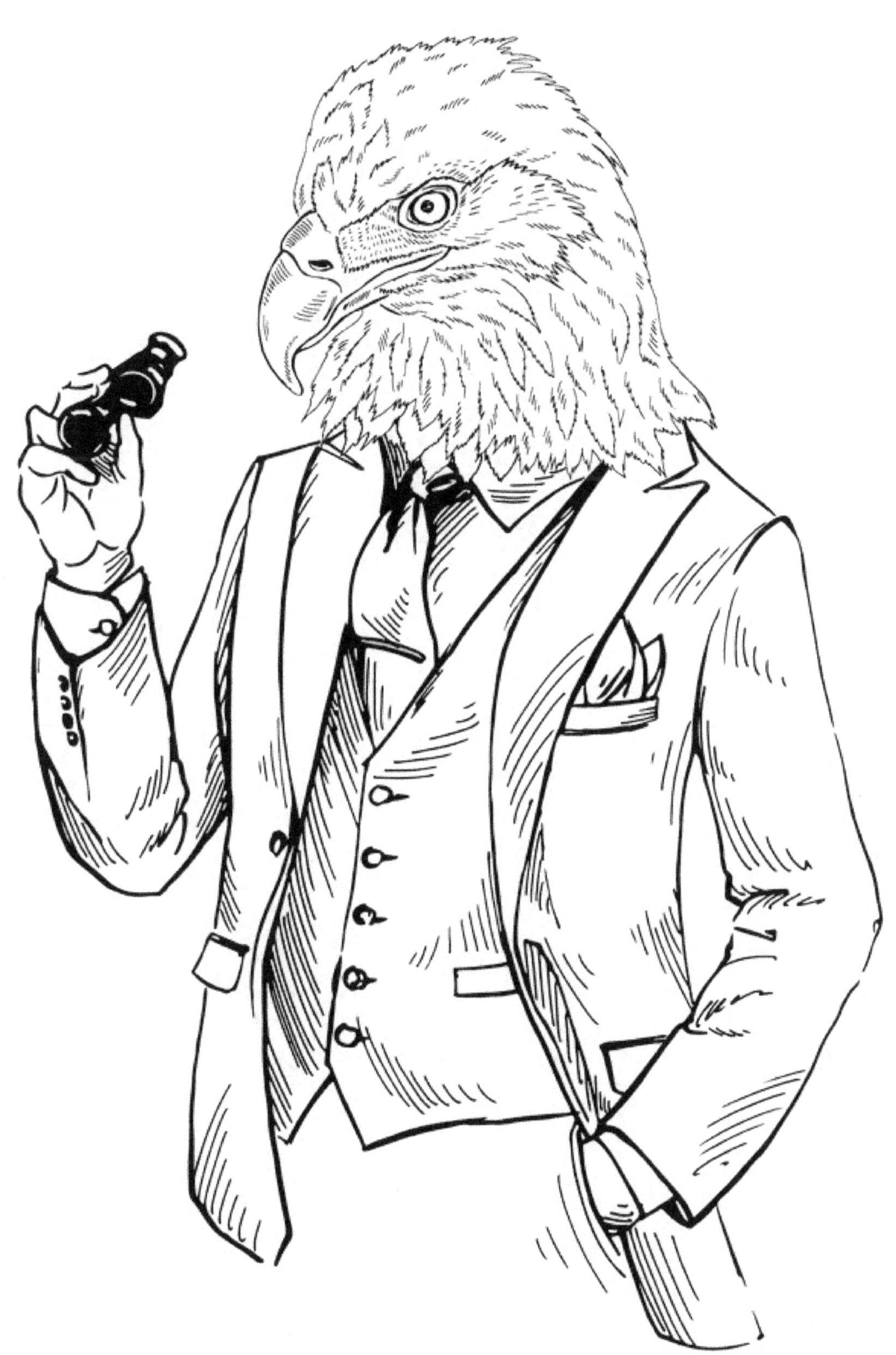

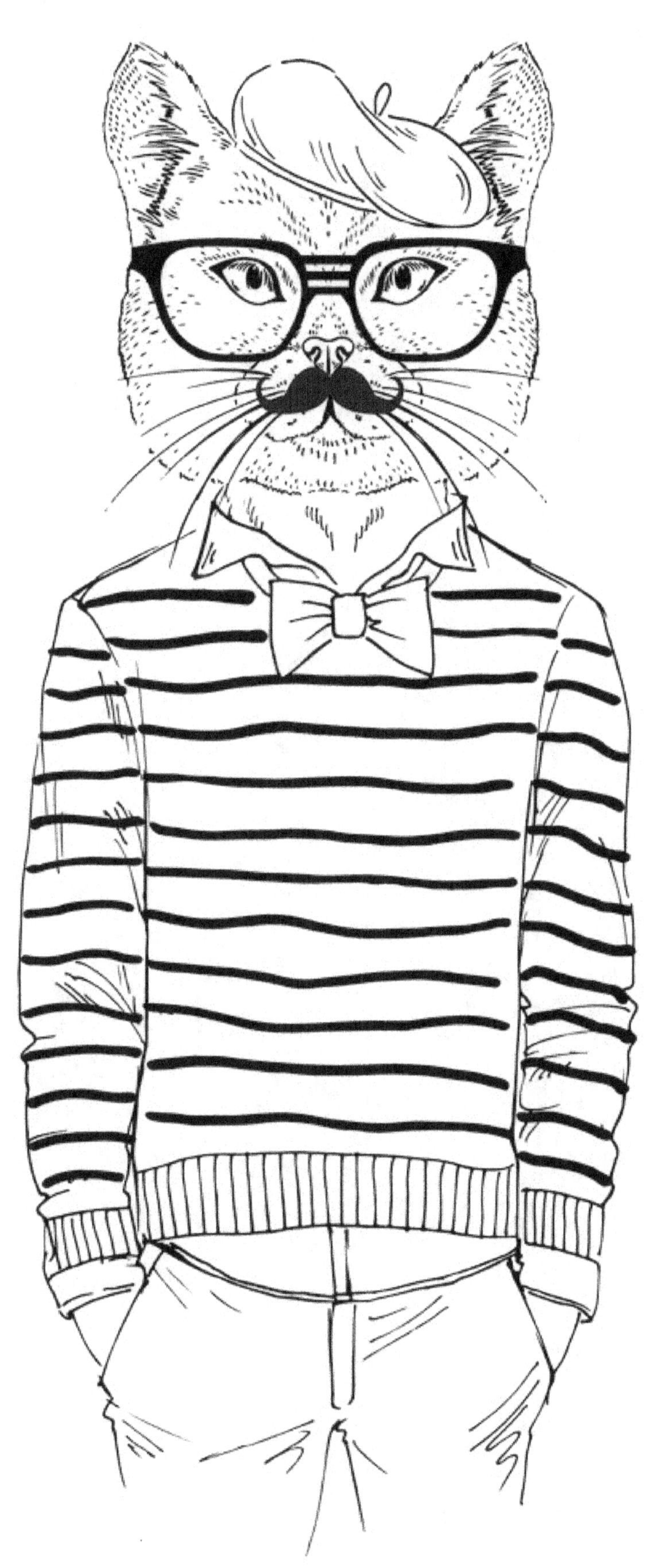

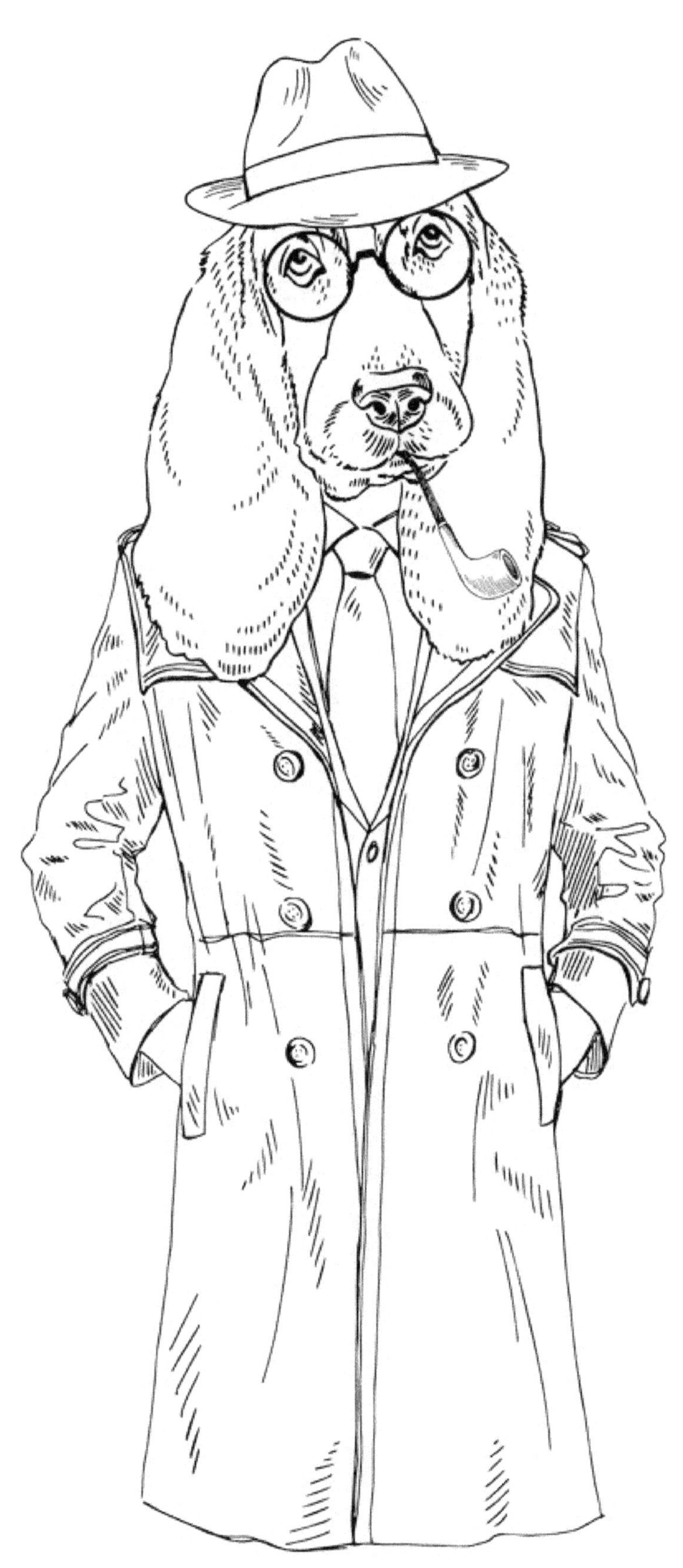

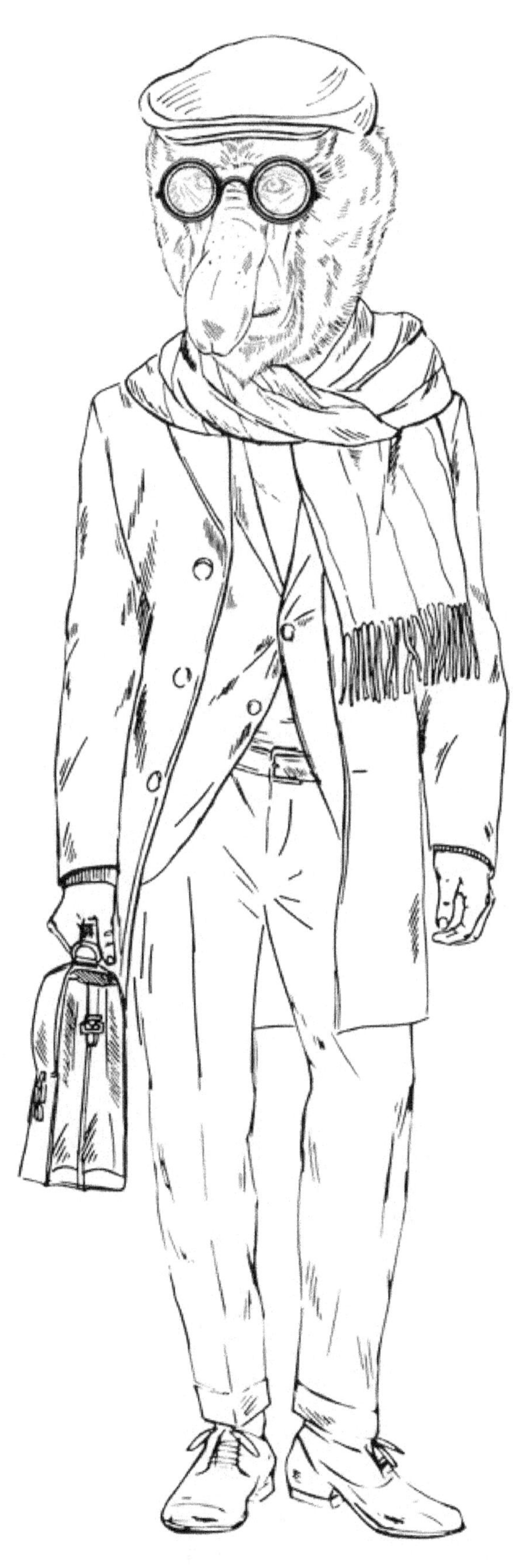

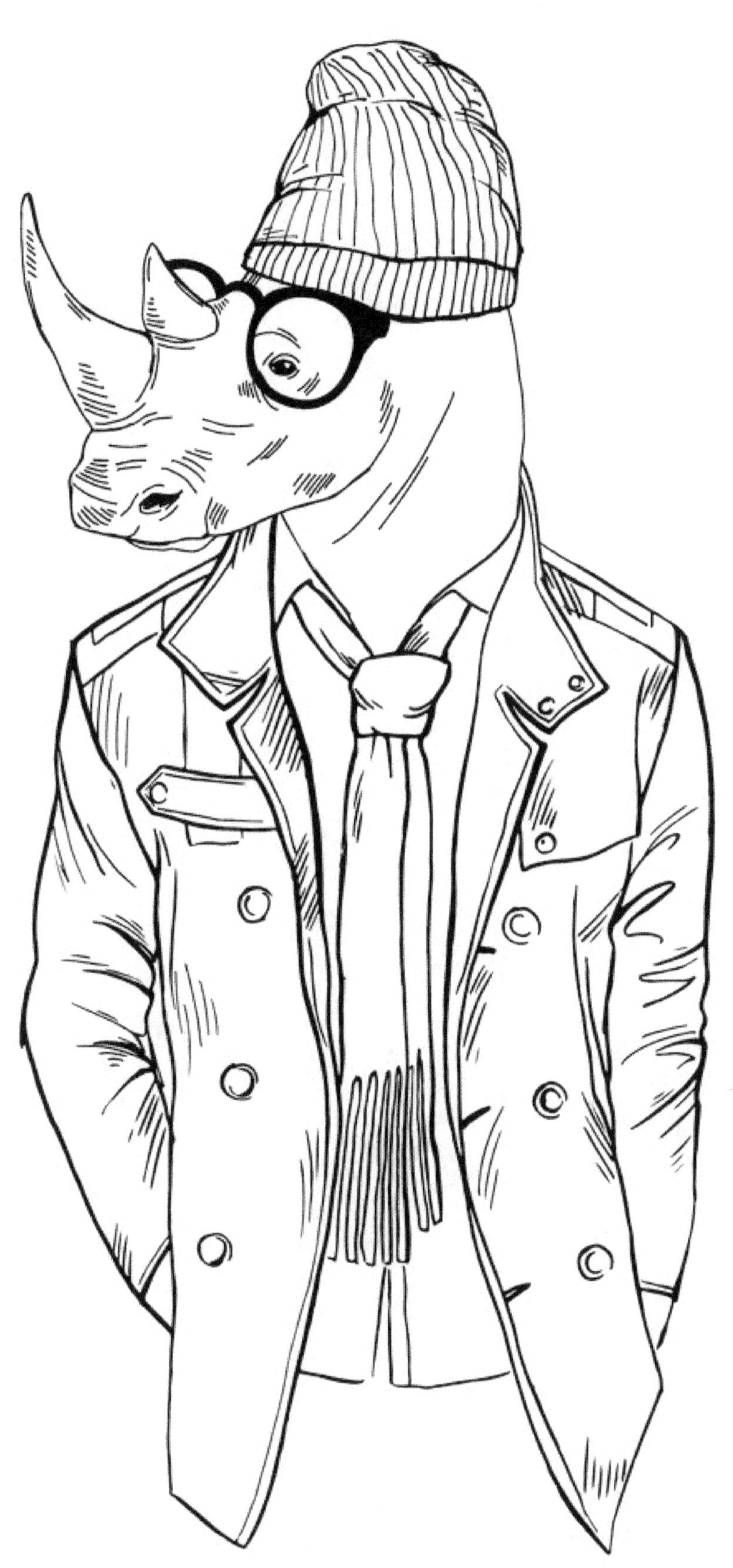

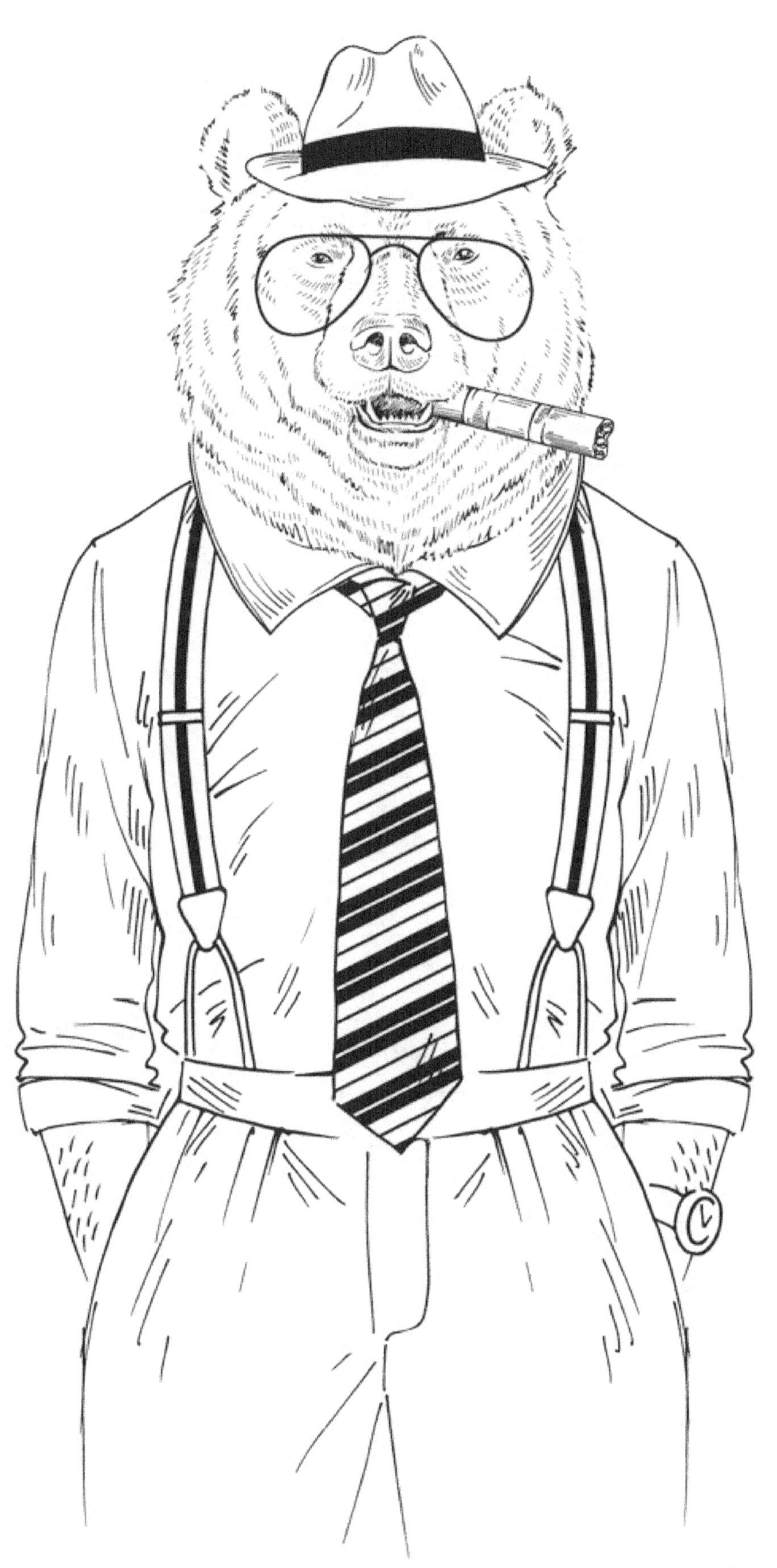

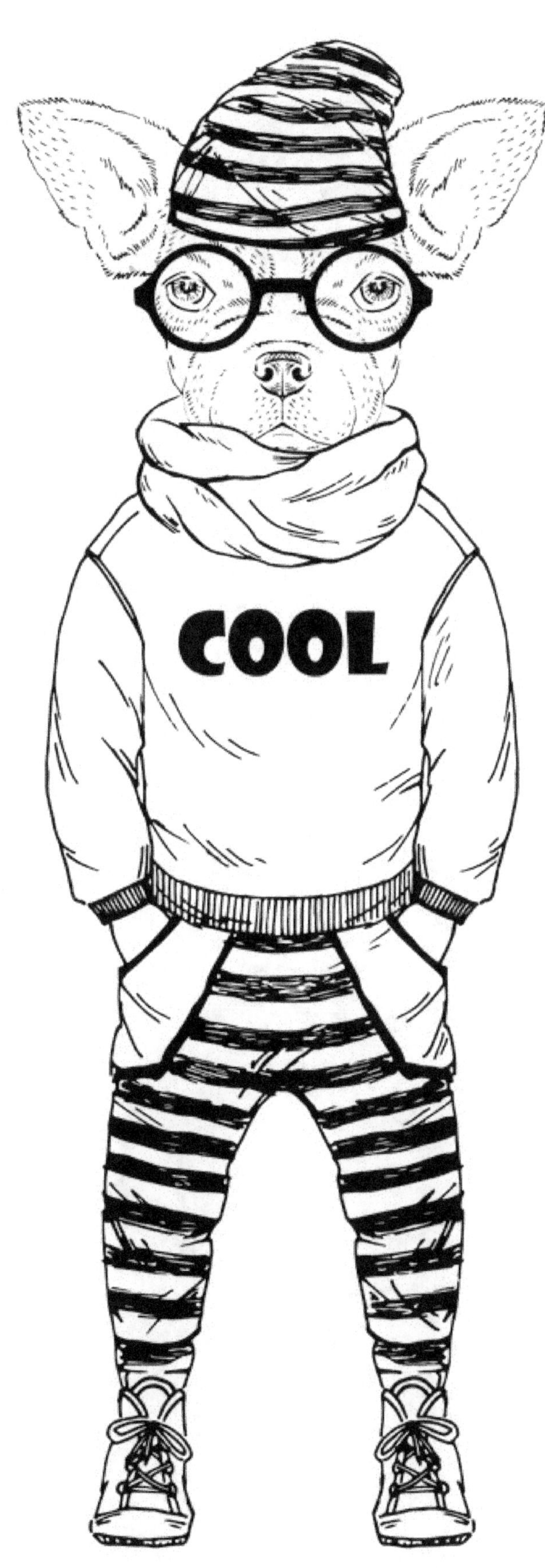
COOL

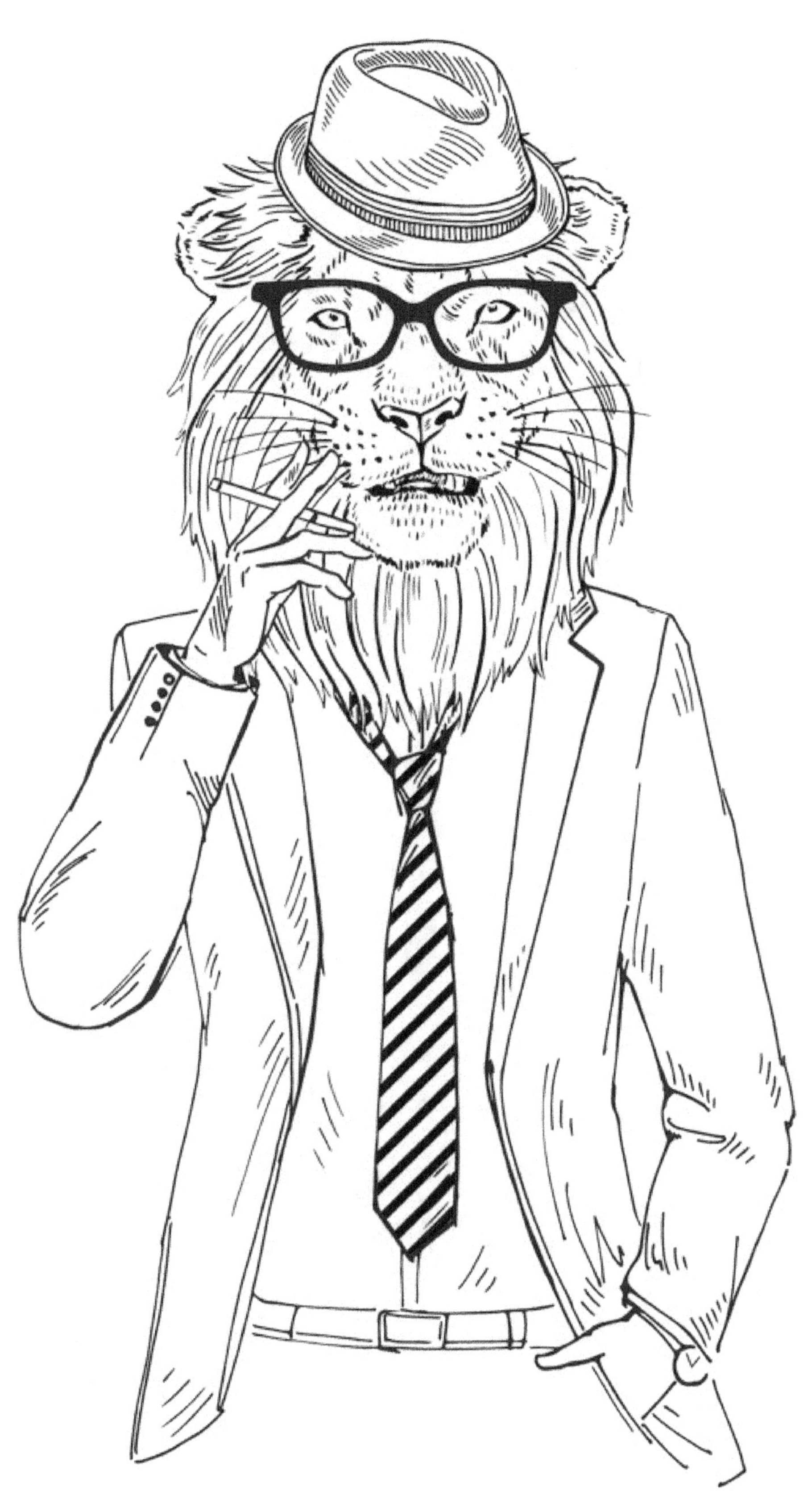

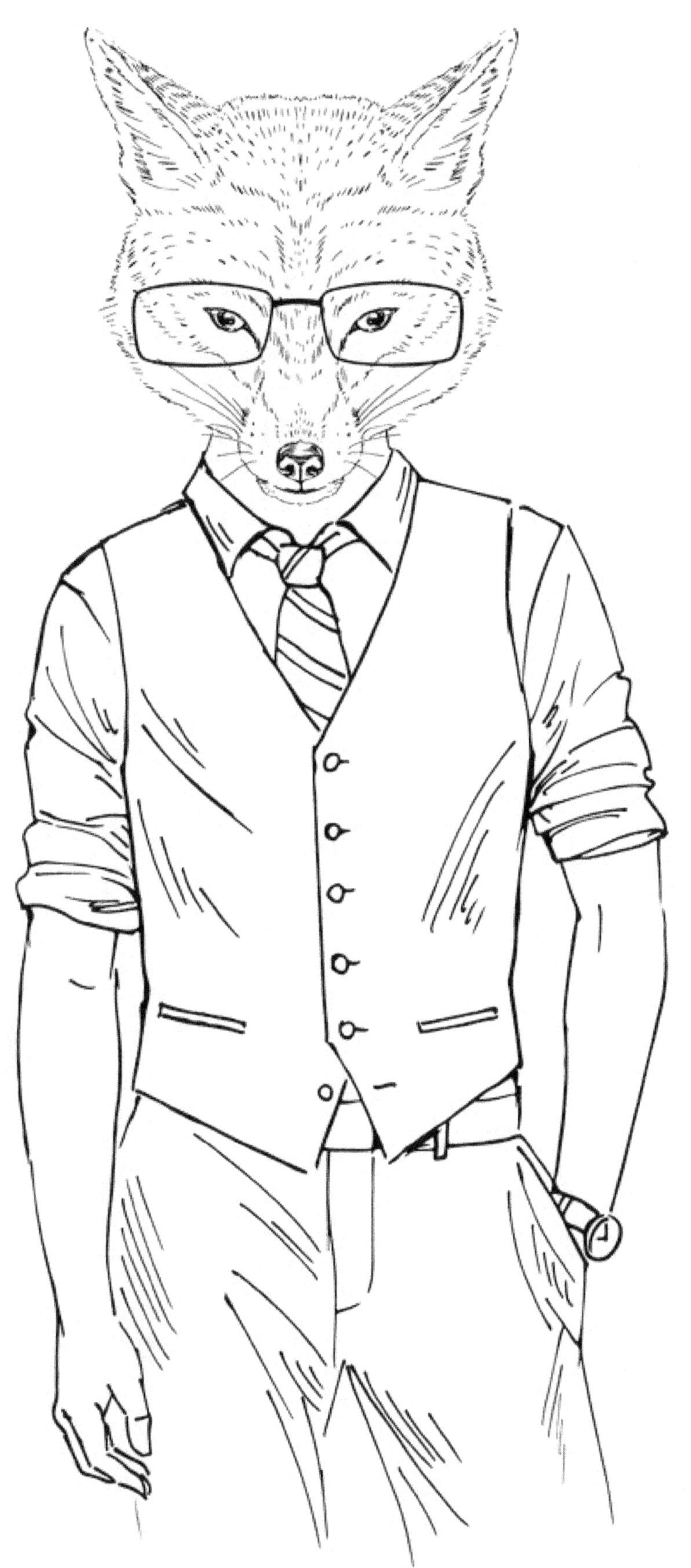

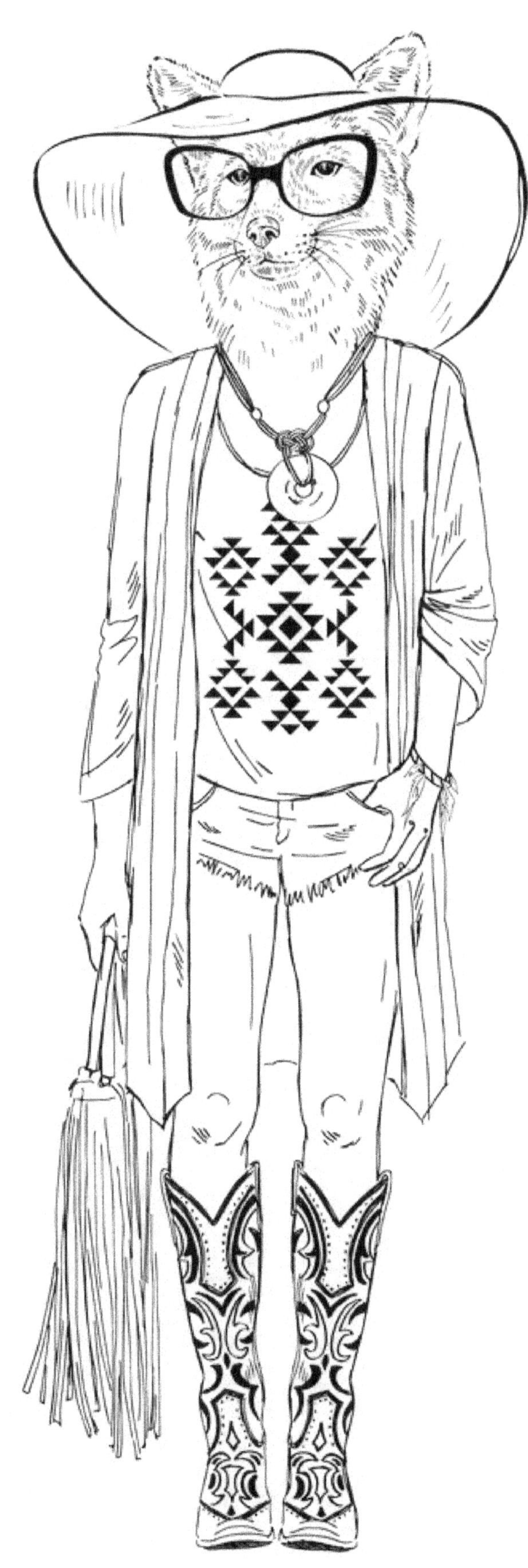

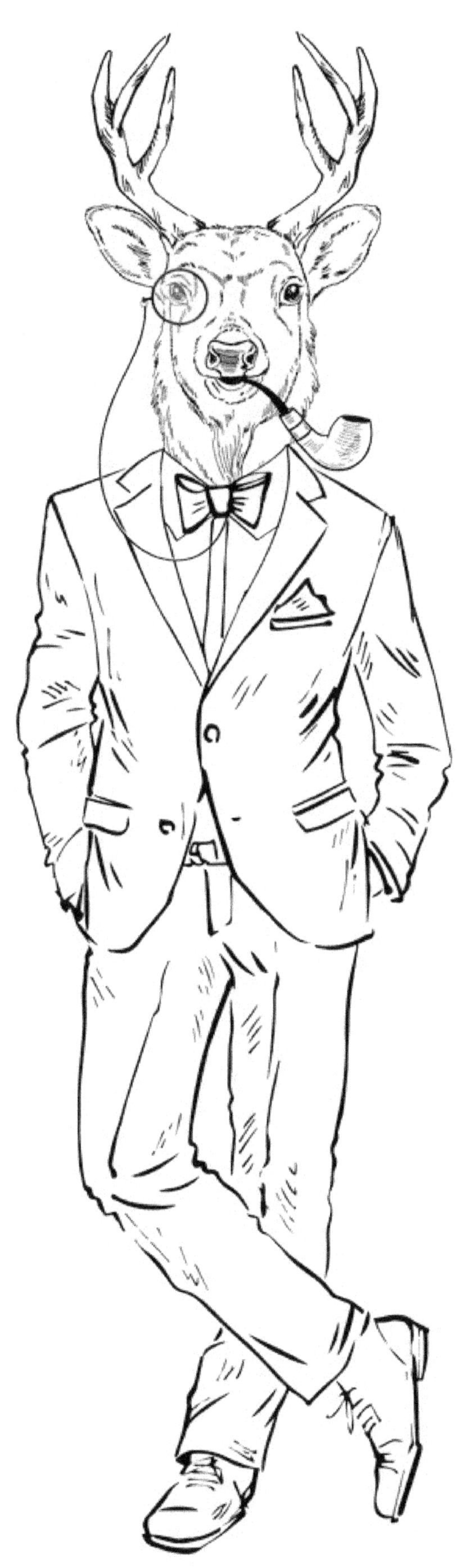

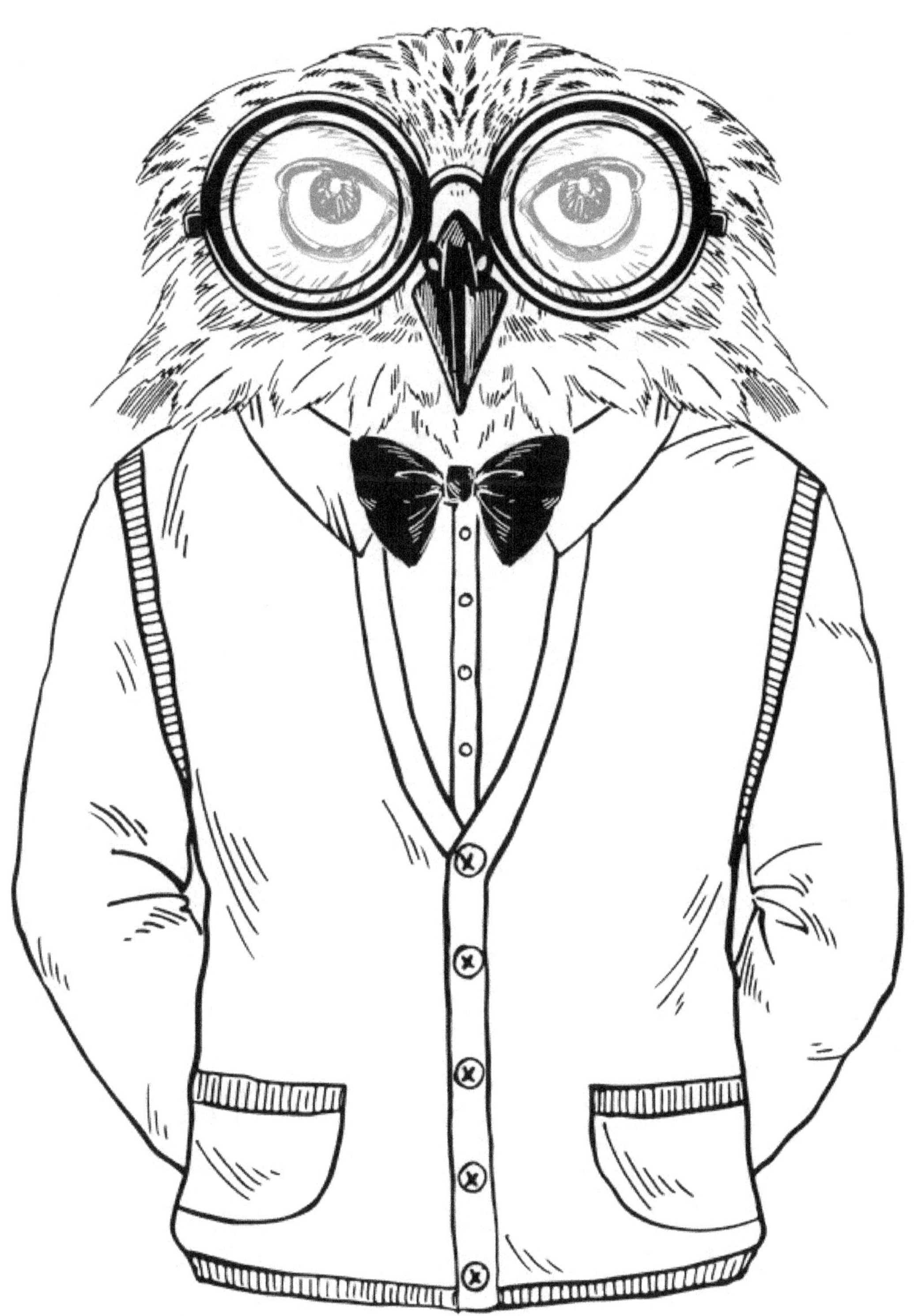

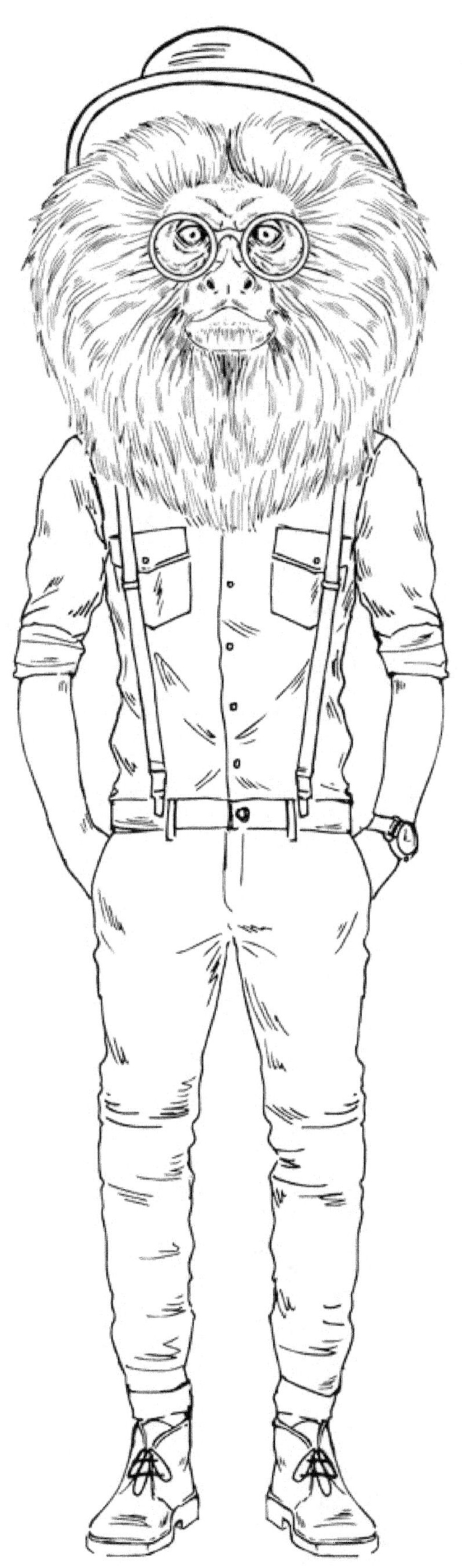

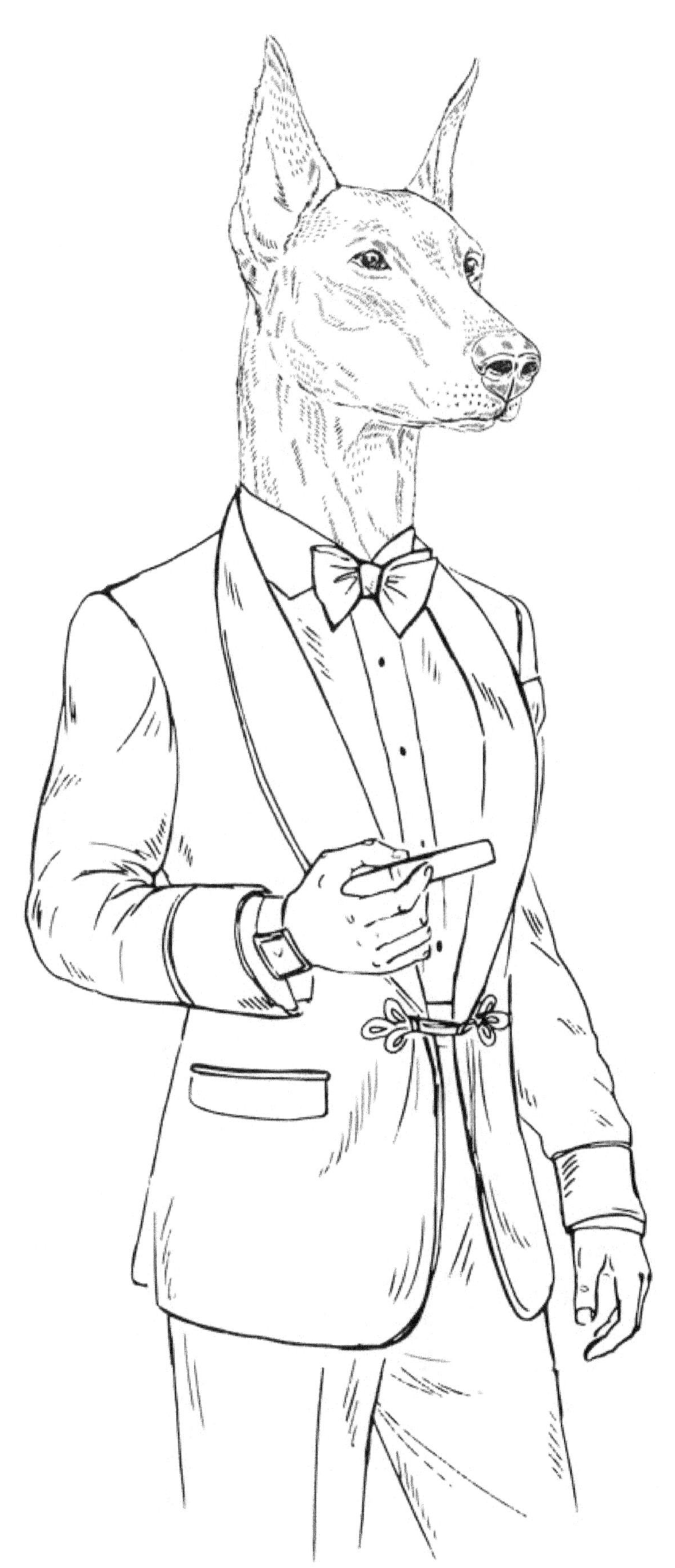

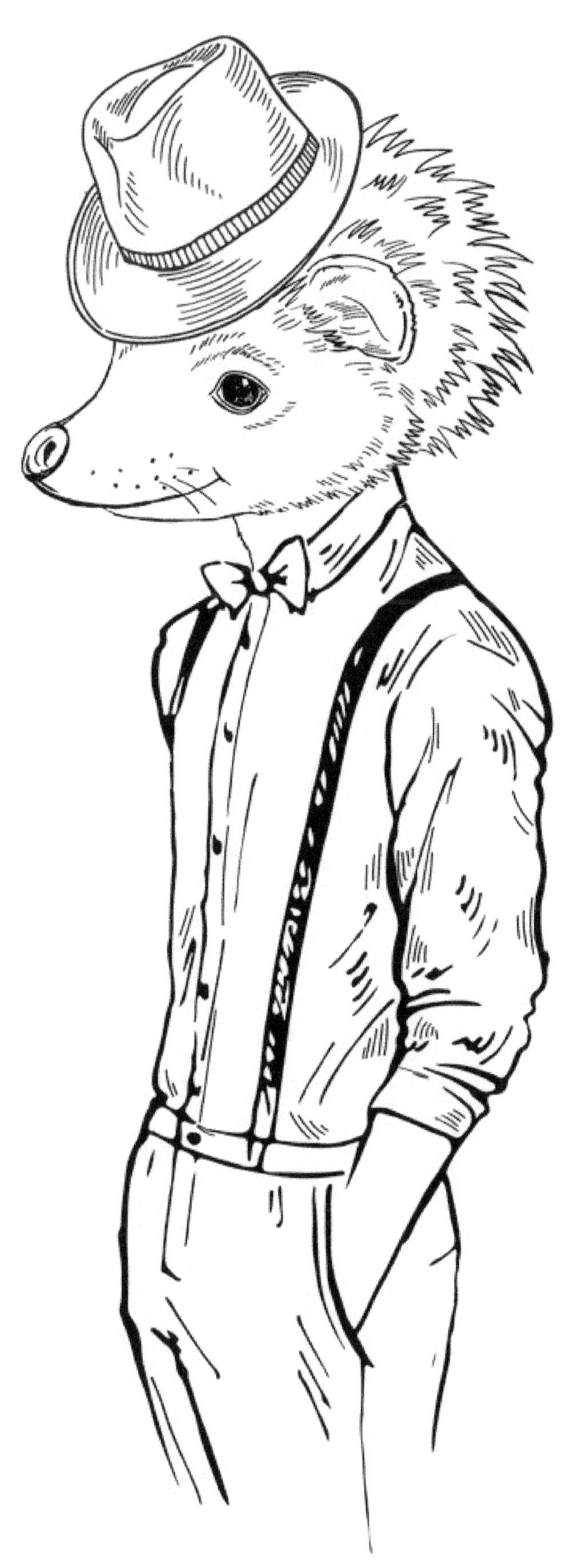

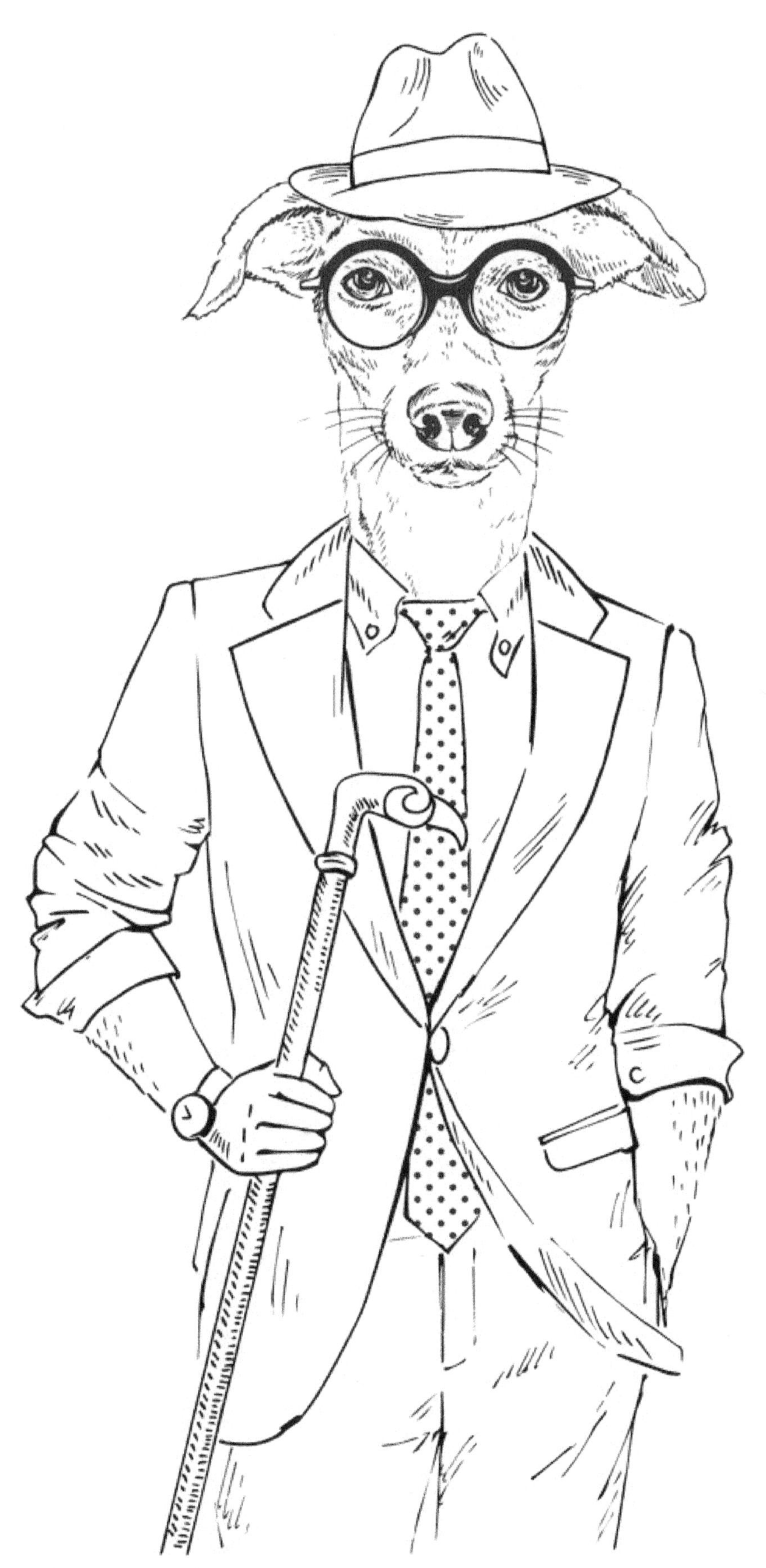

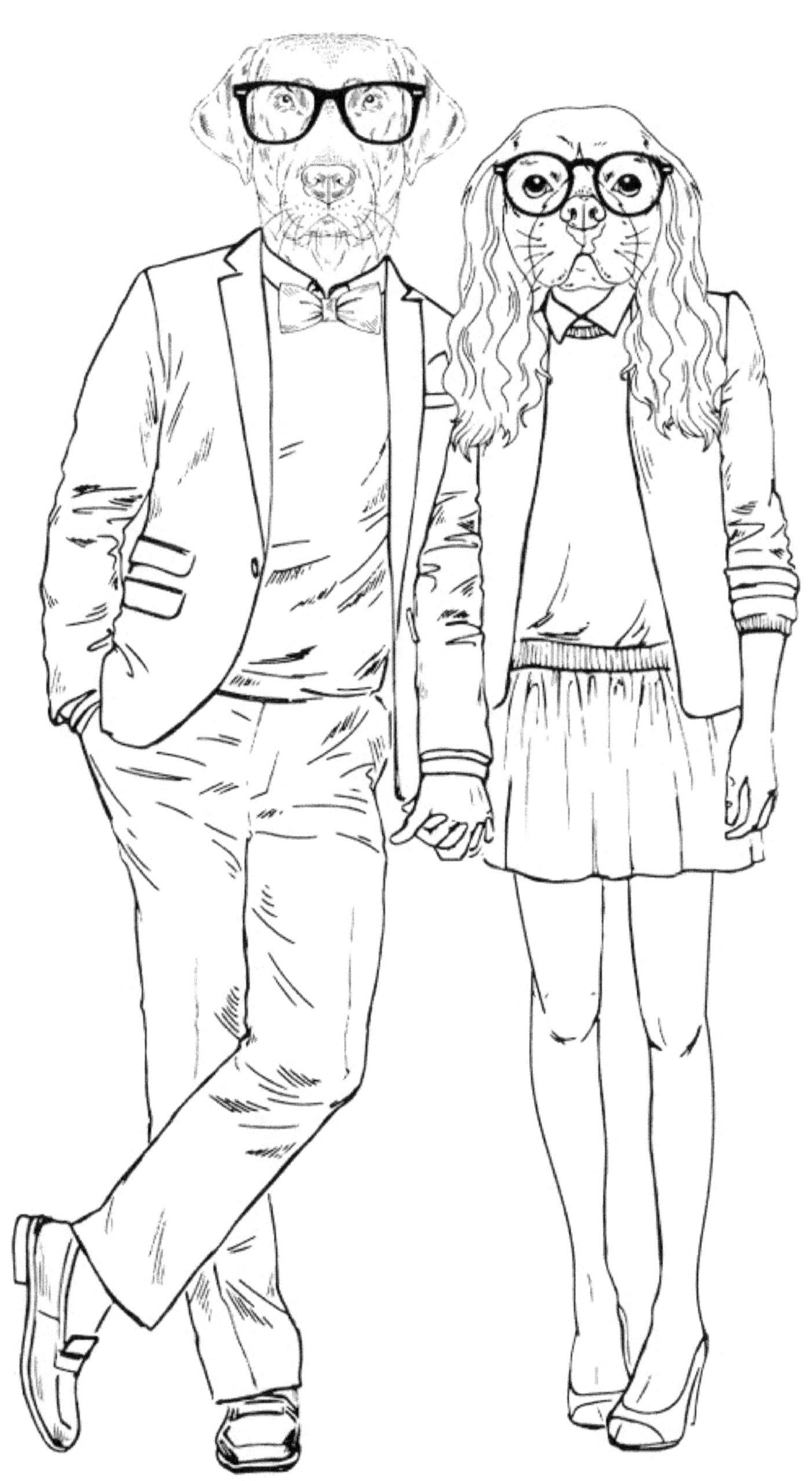

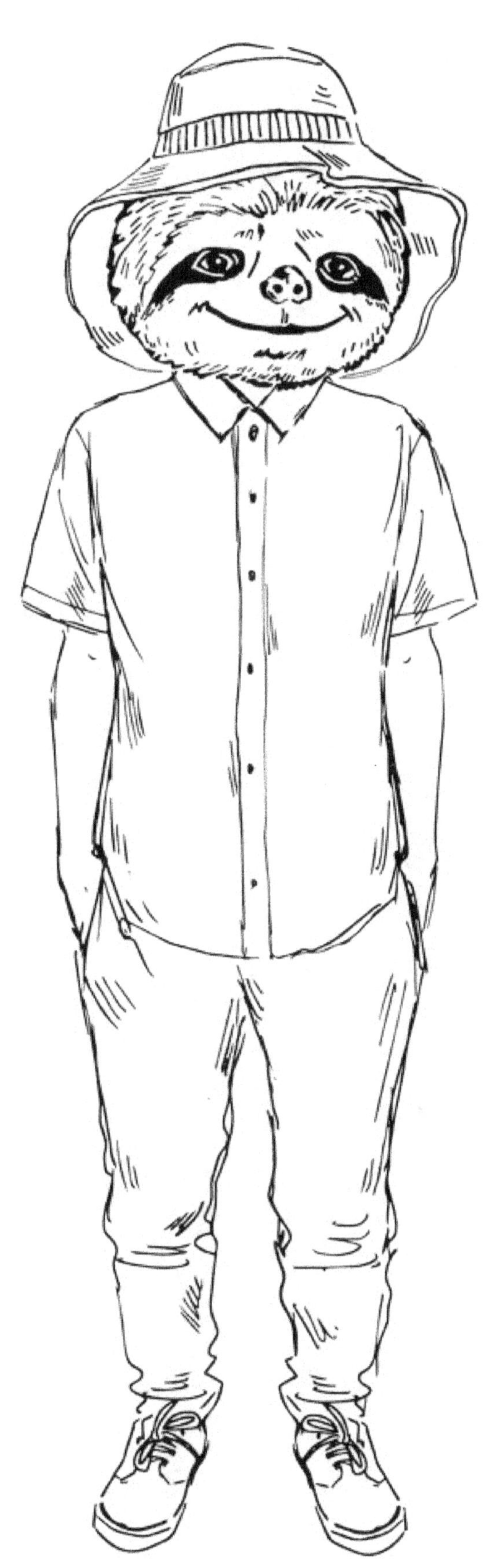

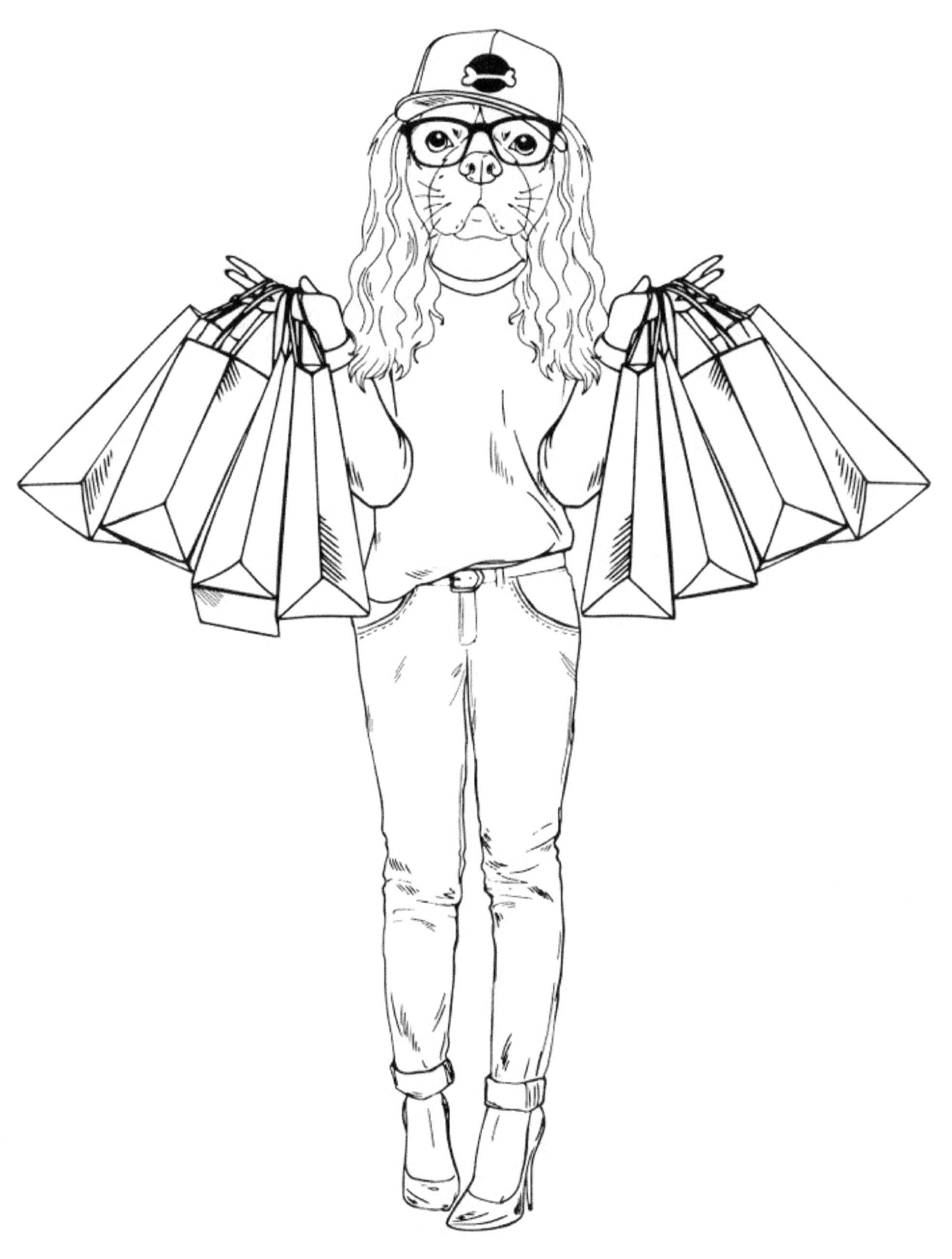

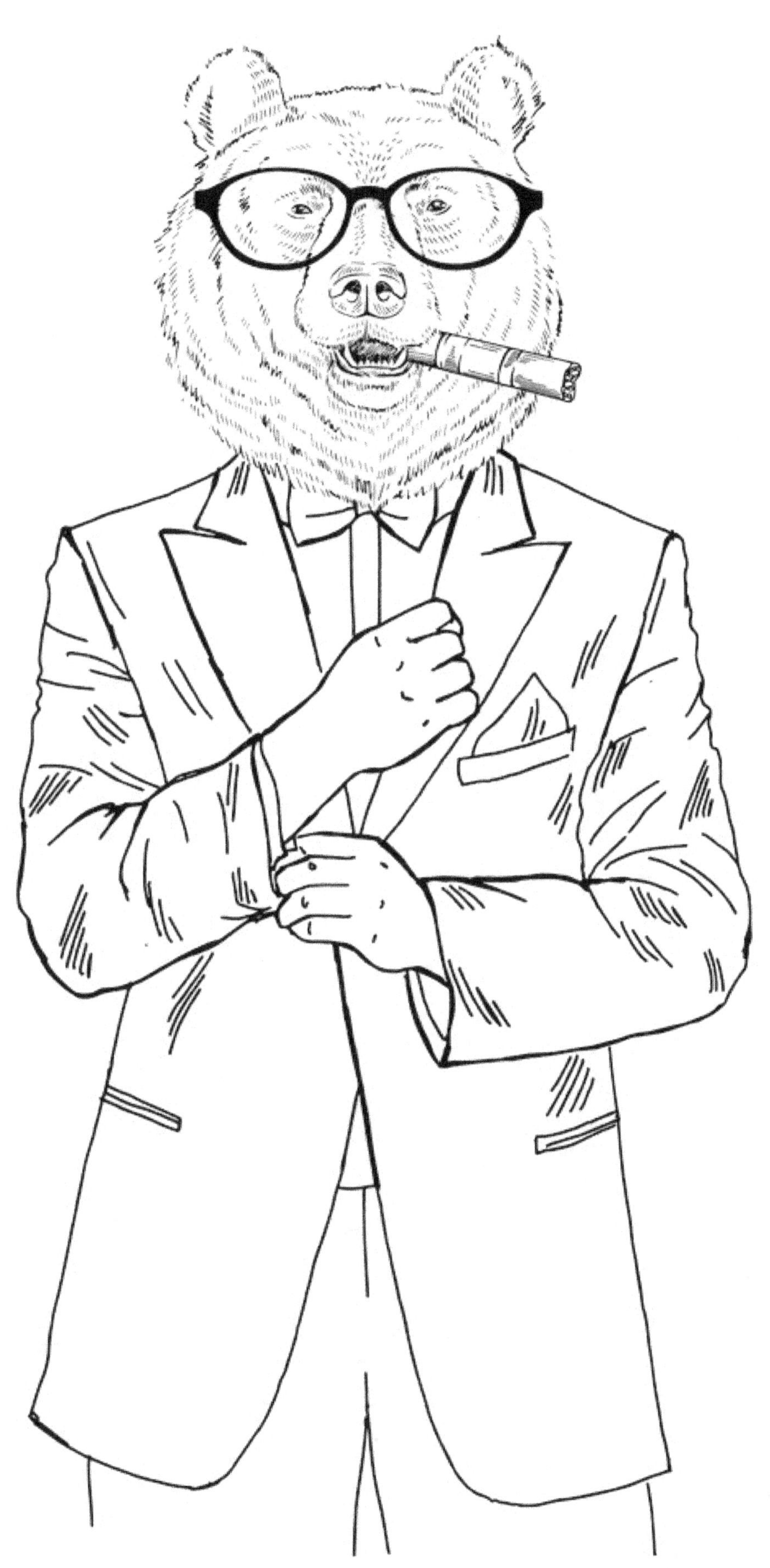

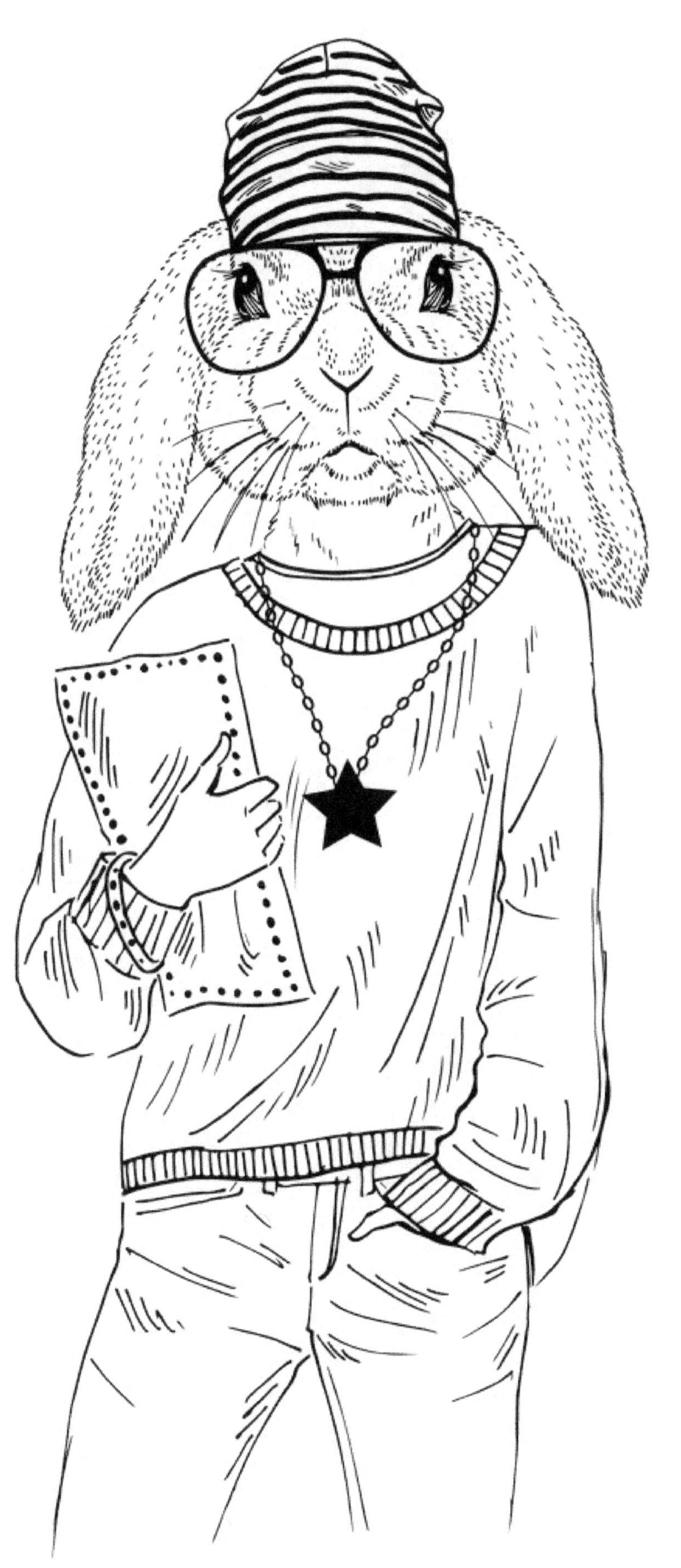

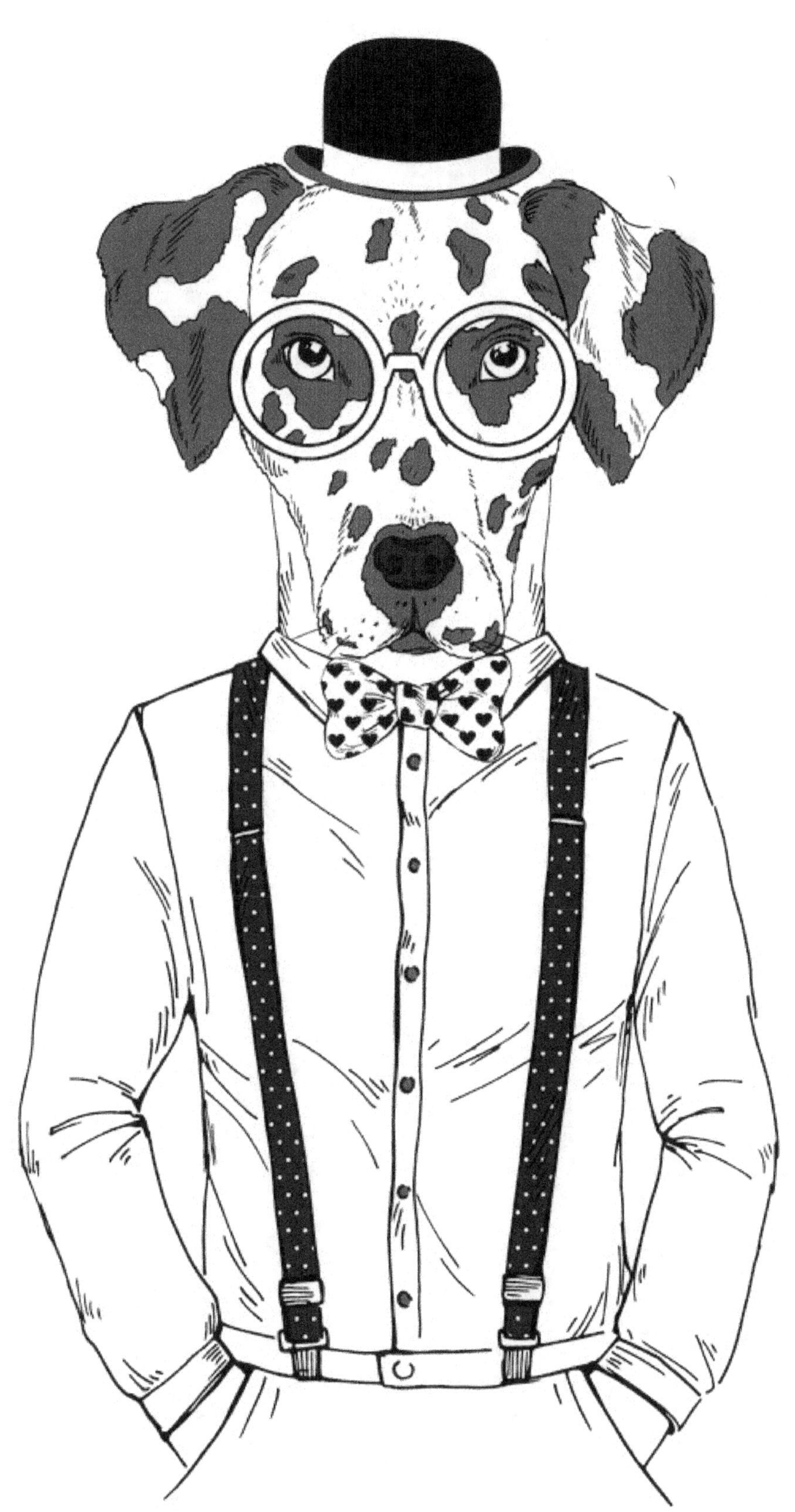

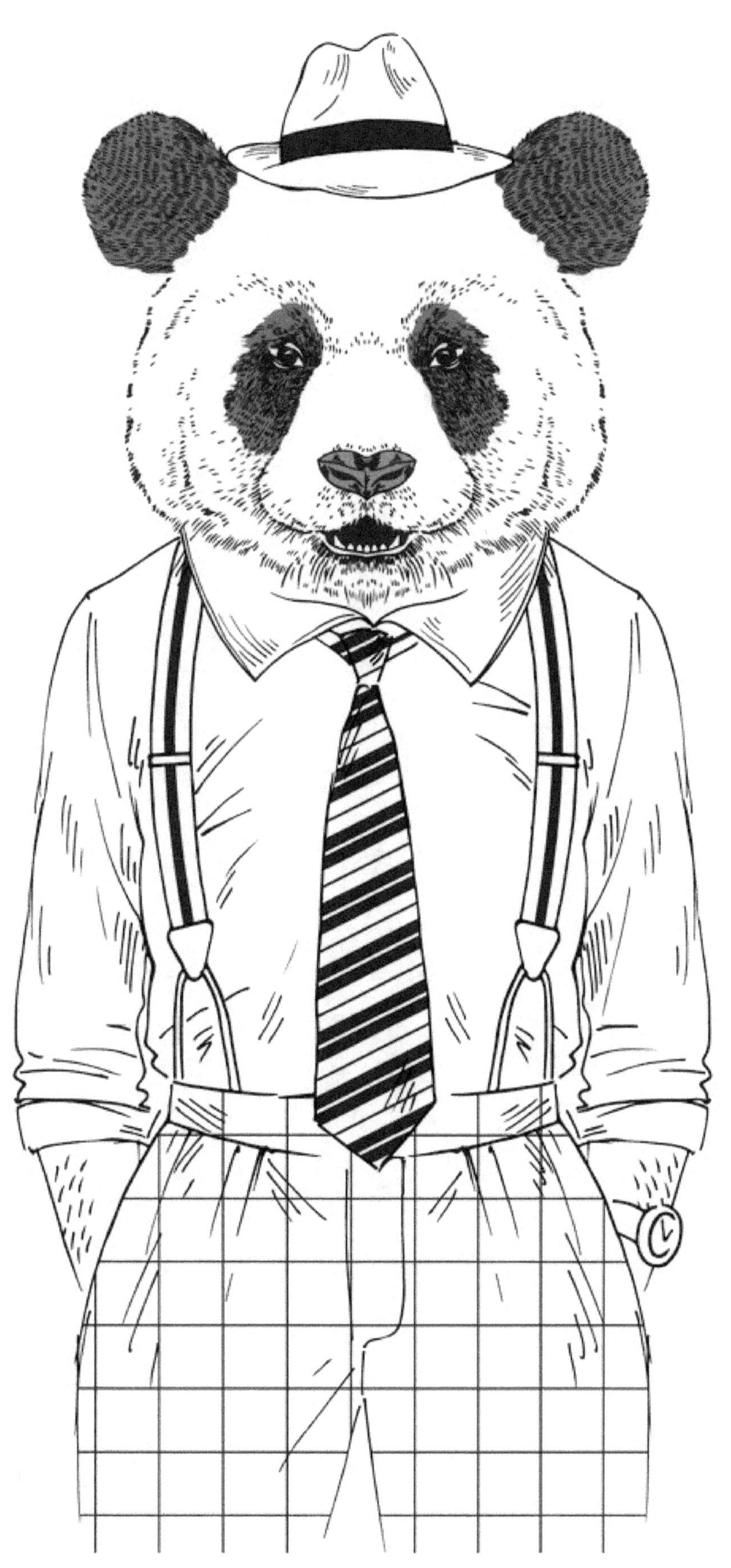

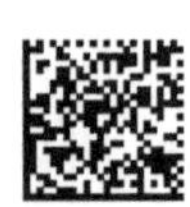